A Billion Bootstraps

Microcredit, Barefoot Banking, and the Business Solution for Ending Poverty

Phil Smith
Eric Thurman

McGraw-Hill

New York   Chicago   San Francisco   Lisbon   London
Madrid   Mexico City   Milan   New Delhi   San Juan
Seoul   Singapore   Sydney   Toronto

The **McGraw·Hill** Companies

2 3 4 5 6 7 8 9 0 DOC/DOC 0 9 8 7

ISBN-13: 978-0-07-148997-3
ISBN-10: 0-07-148997-5

This publication is designed to provide accurate and authoritative information in regard to the subject matter covered. It is sold with the understanding that neither the author nor the publisher is engaged in rendering legal, accounting, or other professional service. If legal advice or other expert assistance is required, the services of a competent professional person should be sought.

—From a Declaration of Principles jointly adopted by a Committee of the American Bar Association and a Committee of Publishers

McGraw-Hill books are available at special quantity discounts to use as premiums and sales promotions, or for use in corporate training programs. For more information, please write to the Director of Special Sales, Professional Publishing, McGraw-Hill, Two Penn Plaza, New York, NY 10121-2298. Or contact your local bookstore.

This book is printed on acid-free paper.

Dedicated to entrepreneurs around the world who,
thanks to microcredit,
are overcoming poverty.

CONTENTS

FOREWORD

In this book, Phil Smith and Eric Thurman discuss some failures of traditional poverty reduction approaches and the successes of the growing microcredit movement from their perspectives as successful entrepreneurs. They have demystified microcredit and given it a human face, as seen through the eyes of two businessmen who are serious about achieving social objectives such as the end of poverty. They have done us a favor by breaking down the challenges of growth for microfinance into bite-sized elements any reader can benefit from, and have challenged and inspired us all to get more involved.

Their pragmatic and business-oriented approach has come up with some useful observations and guidelines for people who are interested in microfinance and are looking for ways to get more involved.

If the goal is to move as many people out of poverty as possible, the focus should be on the poorest of the poor, because then you can help more people by investing the same amount of money.

Despite many advances, including reaching the Microcredit Summit Campaign's goal within one year of the original target date, global poverty persists. Models that rely on government action or capitalism narrowly defined as maximization of financial profit are limited in their ability to put poverty where it belongs—in a museum. The key missing links are grassroots, private sector approaches that focus on the poorest of the poor, but in a way that is businesslike and allows for preservation of investor capital and financial sustainability over time. The potential of "social business enterprises" formed along these lines can make a major impact on the global poverty crisis.

One successful example of a social business enterprise is a microcredit program serving the poor and owned by its poor borrowers. The Grameen Bank project has been working since 1976 and has been a for-profit, member-owned bank since 1983. The bank shows that providing microcredit to the poor can be done in a successful and profitable manner.

Today we have more than seven million borrowers, and 58% of them have already crossed the poverty line and most of the rest are heading in that direction. They have done this through their own efforts, supported by microcredit, microsavings, microinsurances, and a social development program guided by the "16 Decisions" that our clients developed in 1984.

The Grameen Bank is profitable and can expand in Bangladesh with savings provided by the poor (and formerly poor) borrowers and other savers. While the Grameen Bank does not need additional support, other programs in other countries will benefit from support, and Bangladesh can benefit from additional social business investments that improve the lives of the poor. One example of a social business investment is the joint venture with the Danone Group of France (famous for its yogurt products) that will produce and sell fortified yogurt especially formulated for malnourished children in Bangladesh. Another is the eye care hospitals that will bring world class eye care to all levels of the Bangladeshi population with the poor paying less and the richer paying more for identical high-quality services.

I have always maintained that poverty was not created by the poor, but by society's institutions that became a "disabling environment" for them. The Grameen Bank became an "enabling environment" that led to millions of small miracles which, collectively, provide an example of what can be done globally. That the Nobel Prize was awarded this year half to me and half to the Grameen Bank to recognize our progress makes us more committed to reaching new poverty-reduction milestones in the years ahead.

There are many ways people can help microcredit reach its full potential, and this book evaluates some of the most obvious methods—philanthropic support, volunteerism, advocacy, and education. These authors recommend sustainable social business enterprise investments. Depositing savings in a microcredit institution, or in a bank/fund that supports microcredit institutions, is another approach. Additional approaches exist, and, as part of our "Put Poverty into Museums" campaign, the need and opportunity for people around the world to support the growth of this movement is more important than ever.

Phil and Eric have done an admirable job showing us what is happening, what is possible, and what we can do from their perspective as successful business people. I especially like their obvious enthusiasm for investing in the poorest of the poor because doing so will yield the highest return by far in terms of people lifted out of poverty, if not the highest financial return.

Professor Muhammad Yunus
Dhaka, Bangladesh
December 2006

PREFACE

This book grew out of a friendship that developed as Phil Smith, a businessman and donor, asked Eric Thurman, a renowned philanthropy advisor and microcredit expert, to explain how poverty lending works. Phil kept saying, "I have looked and looked, and much of what you are telling me is not available anywhere. Not in print, not on the Internet. This is critical information everyone needs who cares about helping the poor raise themselves from poverty. We should put it in a book." *A Billion Bootstraps* is the result.

Actually, volumes have been written about microcredit, but the material is generally not very inviting or accessible to people who want to learn quickly about this movement that is changing so many lives. Much of what has been written is highly technical for microcredit professionals. Most of the rest underpins the fundraising agendas of individual organizations. We offer an impartial overview of microcredit so you can quickly grasp how it works and discover the many ways to become involved. We write from a business point of view, because poverty responds to the same investment principles that fuel business growth anywhere in the world.

Our goal is to entice thousands more people to join those who already make microcredit a priority in their giving. In face-to-face meetings, we rarely fail to persuade people of the benefits to everyone involved with microcredit, be they poor entrepreneurs or affluent donors. Since we might not visit with you in person, we wrote *A Billion Bootstraps* to accomplish the same purpose. If we reach our goal, more than a billion people will lift themselves from poverty with the help of microcredit.

Acknowledgments

We express our deep admiration for the unsung heroes around the world who operate microcredit programs. The initiative and innovation of these loan counselors is a primary reason why hundreds of millions of people are finding a way out of poverty. Men and women who administer lending programs have been our teachers.

We owe a debt of gratitude to everyone who helped us recast our ideas into a book. Mariann McKinney provided tireless research and helpful critique of the emerging manuscript. Pennie Thurman's skills from years in journalism kept us lucid and on message. Carol Stigger did a masterful job of finding the right words when they eluded us. Carol, we know you could have written that last sentence better than we did. Michael Seidman assisted us greatly in organizing our thoughts and finding the voice to express them. We give special thanks to Lauren Lynch and Herb Schaffner, our editors at McGraw-Hill, for their astute direction and painstaking attention to detail.

Innumerable other people have helped mold our ideas. We thank Bonnie and Dennis Smith, Alan Carlton, Ken Hersh, David Albin, George Kaiser, Steven Dow, Charlotte Beyer, John Barnett, Dave Jewitt, Larry Akers, Courtney Thurman, and Jere Calmes. Rick Warren and Bob Buford inspired us, as they have many others, to find purpose in the second half of life. We are influenced most by God teaching us to love, respect, and value poor people.

We are especially grateful for our wives, Pennie Thurman and Shannon Smith, and the way they encouraged our writing even when it encroached on our personal lives.

Philip B. Smith
Eric B. Thurman

*“ An invasion of armies can be resisted,
but not an idea whose time has come. ”*

—VICTOR HUGO

CHAPTER 1

THE POWER OF WHAT WORKS

Phil Smith

In his spare time, 28-year-old computer scientist Pierre Omidyar created a revolutionary new Web site that eventually became eBay, the largest online auction system of its kind. Omidyar and his wife, Pam, became multibillionaires and philanthropists determined to use their fortune to improve the lives of many. He has said, "Business can make the world a better place and there's no better example of that than microfinance." In late 2005, the Omidyars provided a grant of $100 million to help others begin or improve their businesses. A *Newsweek* article explained the theory behind the gift, "Omidyar has made his largest investments so far in the field of microfinance, which empowers the poor around the world by granting tiny loans (often as small as $50) to poor people who want to become entrepreneurs."

What is this remarkable new method to self-sufficiency that the Omidyars believe in so firmly? What will make it effective in reducing world poverty when governments and international and nongovernmental organizations continue to disappoint in their efforts to find solutions to poverty and its associated problems? If this method works for the Omidyars, can it work for you, too?

Crushing poverty is something that can affect any of us. I remember a time in my own early childhood dominated by the fear of impending poverty; a time when I began to realize that a job was the precarious line between hope and fear. Back then, my father was a geologist in the boom-or-bust oil industry in Oklahoma. Business was so tough in 1958 that in lieu of a Christmas bonus my father received a warning against making any new purchases since his job was at risk. That year I was seven years old. During the remainder of my childhood, I recall my parents whispering as one friend of the family after another lost his job. Throughout that time, I worried that our family was only a phone call away from the hunger and cold I associated with joblessness. As a child, I thought that people lost their jobs because of factors beyond their control and that once unemployed they were destined to a hellish existence; I believed a job was a priceless treasure. As an adult, I am even more convinced this is true.

As an adult, like my father, I was employed in the oil and gas industry and worked hard to protect my family from my childhood fears of poverty. For nearly 30 years I worked long, hard weeks—often sleeping in the backseat of a car surrounded by the noise of a drilling rig—negotiating oil deals in greasy cafés or someone else's luxurious office. By the early 1980s, I was a manager and part owner of a small oil and gas company along with my friend Jim Hays. As the price of oil dropped from $42 per barrel to less than $10 per barrel, the future of that company and our jobs was doomed, and I found myself unemployed. A few years later, Jim purchased a small natural gas pipeline company and offered me a small share of it, which I was able to buy using a $50,000 loan. That loan enabled me to enter the world of those who *bootstrap* their own businesses.

BARON BOOTSTRAP

Baron Münchhausen was a German eccentric who served the Russian military in two campaigns against the Ottoman Empire in the 1740s. Returning home to his manor in Bodenwerder, he acquired a reputation for telling outrageously tall tales about his adventures. According to one such story, he escaped from a swamp by pulling himself up by his own hair. In later versions of that story, the Baron used his own bootstraps to pull himself out of the sea, giving birth to the term *bootstrapping*.

Bootstrappers, as we now know them, are people who build their businesses with sweat equity, not by writing intricate business plans, pursuing investment bankers, or wallowing in market research. Instead, they focus their energy, intelligence, and skills on creating businesses that can thrive in a competitive environment. Bill Gates bootstrapped Microsoft; Masaru Ibuka bootstrapped Sony; and your current financial well-being, like mine, may be based on a business built by you or one of your relatives.

Working with Jim in our new company, I became well acquainted with the sweat equity required to successfully grow a business. Under Jim's guidance, our company went through a whirlwind of mergers and acquisitions. When it was finally merged out of existence, the owners and managers of the company shared a profit of $30 million. With the capital earned from that experience and lessons absorbed in how to run a profitable business, I went on to be a part of a number of other successful business ventures.

In 2002, I ended my career in the oil and gas industry, leaving as CEO and chairman of the board of a publicly traded company whose original investors had received returns of more than three to one in three years. I then chose to begin a new career focused on purposefully living the second half of my life. Wanting to have a direct impact on people's lives, I searched for nonprofit organizations that were financially efficient and where I could make a difference. Unfortunately, finding such organizations turned out to be more difficult than finding oil and gas.

It wasn't until November 2003, sitting in the Dallas/Fort Worth Airport Admirals Club, that I discovered how I could personally make a difference. I had settled into a chair, plugged in my laptop, and begun to check my e-mail. One new e-mail was a thank-you note for a check I had mailed to a charity for the homeless in Tulsa, Oklahoma, where I live. A familiar personal critique of my philanthropic efforts began to nag at me. While I feel that providing the means to shelter the homeless is the right thing to do, the businessman inside me questioned whether this kind of giving was really the most efficient use of my resources. After all, millions of dollars given by thousands of people had not yet solved Tulsa's homeless problem.

Giving money away, I had thought, would be much easier than earning it. I was unaware that experienced philanthropists from Andrew Carnegie to Bill Gates have complained that giving money away is often more difficult than making it in the first place. As a business-minded person, I expect a return on my financial investments. I also expected a different type of return on my giving dollars, such as seeing lives permanently changed for the better, not just temporarily sustained on handouts of food and transient shelter. I wanted to see that folks in all kinds of need were mentored and advised as peers, not patronized as if they were another species, less evolved than men and women in suits and well-polished shoes.

I kept asking myself, "Why is there such a gap between what works in business and the way in which charities operate?" Are these two worlds really so different? In business, outcomes are crucial. It is common sense, not just greed for profit, to focus on the bottom line. It is sound business practice to shut down failing activities and funnel resources to initiatives that are working or show promise. Yet, in the nonprofit world, givers are asked to continue to support projects that don't perform by any objective economic or permanent life change measure.

Headed to the Eternal City, Rome, and the enchantments of two millennia of art and history, not to mention the pleasures of *saltimbocca alla romana*, *gelato*, and *panna cotta*, I determined not to dwell on these thoughts. I helped myself to a soft drink, returned to my chair, and picked up an abandoned copy of the *Dallas Morning News*. I was not expecting anything out of the ordinary, not even that the Cowboys would find a better quarterback. I certainly was not expecting that a cast-off newspaper would eventually send me on an international quest far off the typical tourist track.

The headline of one small article caught my eye and changed my life. "What will a $50 loan buy?" I smiled supposing the proofreader had dropped at least three zeros and was the target of an editor's belated tantrum. But I read on. "A pig, a chicken, a sapling, and more opportunity than Chiapas women ever dreamed possible." The article explained how Lucy Billingsley, a Dallas real estate developer, organized and motivated several hundred Dallas women to raise money for microloans to poor women in Mexico—and changed their lives. What was this about loans? Lending money to people who live in shanties, and expecting them to pay it back? But the women in Chiapas were repaying their loans, starting or expanding their businesses, and sending their children to school as well. Apparently Billingsley had collected hundreds of thousands of dollars to help the poor using a new idea, *microcredit*. This project was clearly different from a typical charity project dedicated to feeding the hungry, treating the sick, and clothing the naked. This was a project that loaned people the money they needed to help themselves and to create a sustainable future.

The difference between my success and that of the women in the article was three zeros. These women were substantially improving their lives with sweat equity and $50 loans. I had improved mine with sweat equity and a $50,000 loan. I recalled what my father said each time I launched a new company: "Phil, engineers and other professionals like you are a dime a dozen. What really makes the world go around is capital. Without capital, businesses cannot grow."

With growing excitement, I reread the article to make sure my conclusion was accurate: with capital and sweat equity, poor people can change their lives. Bootstrapping is something all of us can benefit from; it has global application. And, judging by Billingsley's project, it works. The $50 I had spent on Italian CDs for the plane ride could change an impoverished family's life, not just put a new roof on their shanty that might blow away during the next hurricane.

I began to investigate microcredit as soon as I returned home from my trip. For several months my assistant, Mariann, and I mined the Internet and searched bookstores and libraries while growing increasingly frustrated. We read microcredit success story after success story, from a tailor in the Dominican Republic who, prior to his microloan, sewed baby blankets and diapers because he could not afford enough cloth to make even one man's suit, to a mother in India who, thanks to a $25 microloan, made enough straw brooms to buy her children back from bonded servitude. We silently congratulated each microentrepreneur, but all the information we found was either written for microcredit professionals or to raise money for microcredit organizations. We were trying to learn about the nuts and bolts of microcredit and how it works on a practical level rather than just esoteric lending practices and heart-rending stories. We wanted to know how microcredit works so it could be efficiently applied to new situations, and we wanted to understand why what is working so well in developing countries is not being used to help the poor in developed countries.

Finally, Mariann handed me a *Forbes* magazine opened to an article titled, "Contrarian Charity: you want big returns on your investments, so why not on your charitable giving, too?" The article profiled Eric Thurman, a world leader in philanthropy and microcredit. I called Eric, who was busy, but not too busy to talk about microcredit and investment philanthropy. Eric is rarely too busy to talk about those subjects, because he has seen them change lives in more than 30 countries. He knows how they work and why they work.

As we talked, I kept expecting to have my wallet opened with the pry bar of guilt. When was Eric going to agonize out loud about overcrowded orphanages and e-mail me photos of children with bloated bellies? But Eric kept the focus on microcredit and explained how a little working capital in the hands of a basket weaver in Uganda produces a sustained income increase, not just her family's next meal. I was astonished to finally understand how people acquire the power to turn a shriveled, stricken economy in Indonesia into a vibrant community where children go to school, health and nutrition improve, and poverty-driven horrors like starvation and prostitution are memories, not the future.

Eric said that many people share the concerns I had raised regarding the fate of the indigent in developed countries, using the rationale that the lives of basket weavers in Uganda are equal in value to those of our next-door neighbors. But unfortunately, he explained further, microcredit, which works so well in developing countries, does not appear to work equally well in developed ones, and he suggested that I do the math to enable me to understand why.

I delved into the new information and built databases and spreadsheets. I worked through equations honed by microcredit experts, and then created my own. They all led to the same conclusion: By focusing their giving dollars on microcredit loans in developing nations instead of on charities in the developed world, givers multiply the impact of their donations by much more than 100 times.

Still, as much as I wanted to believe it, I was not convinced that my giving could help eliminate, not just stick a bandage on, hunger, child trafficking, the spread of AIDS, and every other poverty-related problem. I told Eric that microcredit sounded too good to be true, that the cost of helping people in developing nations seemed unrealistically low when compared to the money being spent helping people in my own community. I also expressed my disbelief that such a simple idea could actually solve problems, not just provide temporary relief or the promise of far-off cures like most of the charities I was used to dealing with. We agreed to meet over dinner in Philadelphia to further discuss the issue.

We went to one of Eric's favorite Indian restaurants. "Look at microcredit this way," he said. "You have all you need because you have a job that gives you financial security. If you lose your job, the government will take care of your basic needs for food, shelter, and healthcare."

"After a lot of paperwork," I noted.

Eric passed the *naan*. "It takes a lot to weave nationwide social safety nets," he said, "which poor countries don't have." He explained that in those countries people work hard to weave their own safety nets, but this is difficult when millions of people do not even make enough money to stave off hunger.

Eric continued, "You can do something about it. You. Not the government. Not the United Nations. Not the experts with the Ph.Ds."

"I've noticed that they haven't eliminated poverty," I said. Eric replied "That's because poverty is about money. Who knows how to handle money? Business people. And, the more successful they are in business, the more creative they can be in philanthropy. Many things cause poverty, but one common thread is that there is absolutely no access to capital in poor countries, and without capital the people and their societies have no chance to grow their businesses."

Remembering that my father had made the same observation, I pushed my half-eaten food aside and handed my notebook to Eric. "My calculations show that I can help put thousands of people on the road to economic improvement by investing in a good microcredit program."

"And in turn each of those people supports at least five family members." Eric responded. "But you can do even better than that." He took a pen from his shirt pocket and jotted a number on a napkin.

Too many zeros, I thought. "How can a person like me help that many people lift themselves from poverty?" I asked.

"That's after your initial investment has been at work for several years," Eric said, "and after we do some financial engineering."

Before the dinner check arrived, I was comfortably applying the same investment principles to philanthropy as in leveraged buyouts, IPOs, and hedge funds. I grew comfortable that the same principles that bring success in the financial world could be applied to helping develop the economies of poor countries anywhere in the world. I finally understood how investments in humanity could yield astonishing returns.

Microcredit is well on its way to changing the world. Innovators like the Omidyars and Bill and Melinda Gates, along with political figures such as former President Clinton and celebrities like actor Brad Pitt, have discovered that microcredit is a powerful tool that can be used to solve many of humanity's most difficult problems. It is so powerful that the impact of microcredit on poor families and communities around the world already goes far beyond typically held views of what is possible. Microcredit makes common sense, and its impact is measurable both financially and in terms of lives changed.

Learning about microcredit and ways that microcredit organizations can leverage contributions has become my personal passion. I can now see how tiny loans can change the destiny of more than a billion of the world's working poor. I have made it my personal mission to help at least 1 million of them start bootstrapping themselves out of poverty!

NOBEL PRIZE WINNERS

In this millennium, the Nobel Peace Prize has recognized efforts, such as microcredit, that foster development and peace. In 2002 the Nobel Peace Prize went to former U.S. President Jimmy Carter, Jr., for finding peaceful solutions to international conflicts, advancing democracy and human rights, and promoting economic and social development. In 2003, Shirin Ebadi won the award for her efforts for democracy and human rights, and in 2004 Dr. Wangari Maathai won the Nobel Peace Prize for her contribution to sustainable development, democracy, and peace. Then, in 2006 the Nobel Peace Prize was awarded to a microcredit pioneer, Dr. Muhammad Yunus and the Grameen Bank.

With 3 billion people living on less than $2 per day, I knew I needed to share both the problem and the solution with more people than I could talk to in person. So, two years ago I asked Eric to join me in writing this book. Shortly before this book went to press, Dr. Muhammad Yunus and the Grameen Bank, of which he is the founder, were awarded the 2006 Nobel Peace Prize for pioneering work in microcredit. Finally, microcredit is headline news, an idea whose time has come.

" *To give away money is an easy matter*
and in any man's power. But to decide to whom
to give it, and how large, and when,
and for what purpose and how, is neither in
every man's power nor an easy matter. "

—ARISTOTLE

CHAPTER 2

BEYOND THE $900 BILLION BLACK HOLE

Eric Thurman

Do you put money in Salvation Army Christmas kettles? Respond to disaster appeals? Volunteer at a local library or hospital? Leave change in a street musician's guitar case? One way or the other, most people are donors. The only difference among us is how much we give and in what ways. Some people make only incidental contributions, such as those mentioned above. Others, such as Phil Smith, put serious energy and thought into their giving. Phil is someone I met as he was pursuing his giving options with all the tenacity of a person hot on the trail of an exciting major investment.

Other than the likelihood that you are a giver at some level, I can also predict, with a high probability of accuracy, that you possess a second trait related to giving. You are cynical, or at least occasionally concerned, about whether the money you donate is used well or has much impact. Many of us are caught in this double-bind of wanting to give, but being haunted by doubts as to whether our contributions make much real difference. Healthy cynicism is a virtue. Let it be a constructive force that motivates you to make better giving decisions.

My career has included a mix of owning businesses and running enterprises for others, serving as an active donor, and managing tens of millions of philanthropic dollars for foundations and individuals. My extensive experience leading philanthropic organizations includes supervising microcredit programs in more than 30 countries and directing grant making for a wide range of programs in 102 nations. In short, I have spent the bulk of my career at the intersection of business and philanthropy.

This intersection is lightly traveled despite the magnitude of nonprofit activity, which is $900 billion of capital in motion annually in the United States alone. You might think that charity finances and sound business practices merge naturally, but that has unfortunately not often been the case. Those signposts that routinely mark the path to success in business are often missing on the charity highway. An example of this contrast between the approaches used in nonprofit versus for-profit business practice is the fact that almost all charitable giving is defined solely by the amount involved; seldom are other factors considered. Any savvy business person knows that price alone does not define whether a deal is good. Attention to detail can reveal that a cheap price is not a bargain and, alternatively, that sometimes a higher price can be a better value. Even more significant is that business has reliable ways of determining when a transaction is desirable.

One principle deal makers know is that the structure of a transaction can be every bit as important as the face value. This point was driven home for me in the early 1990s when I was CEO of a leading microcredit organization, Opportunity International. Our office was in a small, suburban business park with two tower buildings that seemed identical in every way. One day I was notified by our leasing agent that the landlord of our building was going bankrupt, but that, thankfully, it would not affect our building. The problem was that the financial basis of the other tower, also owned by our landlord, was no longer viable. I discovered that while the offices in our building were rented to tenant companies, the other tower's office suites had been sold to companies as condominiums. Unfortunately, that arrangement had not been a sound business decision. Our landlord's financial problems were eventually resolved without affecting us. The incident, however, became instructive about how critical terms and details are in any major financial transaction. As the business adage says, "Of course we can do business. You can set the price if I can set the terms or vice versa." In business you are likely to end up with the short end of the stick if you fail to give as much heed to the details of a transaction as you do to the price.

The discipline of thinking about such details is not nearly as common in the charitable world as in business—and that discipline is badly needed. Following it will make you a better donor and, ultimately, force charities to achieve better results. The trend of business leaders adopting philanthropy as a top priority has been positive in large part because of the business acumen they bring to their giving. They base their decisions on the results expected and insist on knowing how their donations will be used. Only then do they decide the amount they will give. This is tremendous progress for donors, for charities, and for the people they wish to help.

When Warren Buffett announced he would direct more than $30 billion of his philanthropy through the Bill & Melinda Gates Foundation, headlines shouted the amount. Only a few news reports noted an important stipulation he put on the contribution. His money could not be treated as an endowment for the Gates Foundation; rather, it had to produce a result in the programs that was commensurate with the amount donated. The way in which Buffett structured the transaction significantly changes its impact. Gates and Buffett are leading the way for twenty-first century philanthropists by applying business principles to their giving.

The theory of investing that propelled Warren Buffett to wealth and fame is in fact highly transferable to giving. Buffett formed his core investment philosophy under the tutelage of Benjamin Graham, known as the Dean of Wall Street in the late 1940s when he studied under him at Columbia University, earning the only A+ the famed professor ever awarded. In 1949 Graham published his landmark book *The Intelligent Investor*. Buffett says, ". . . it was by far the best book about investing ever written. I think it still is." Graham begins his book by exhorting buyers to distinguish between *investment* and *speculation*. He writes, "We must prevent our readers from accepting the common jargon which applies the term 'investor' to anybody and everybody in the stock market. . . . What do we mean by 'investor'? Throughout this book the term will be used in contradistinction to 'speculator.'" A few pages later, Graham uses even stronger language when he adds the word *gambling* to his discussion of speculation. He warns that such practices can be seductive. "Speculation is always fascinating, and it can be a lot of fun." Graham says people are speculating and even gambling at times when they think they are investing. What is the nature of actual investing? Good analysis is what defines investment while "operations not meeting these requirements [of good analysis] are speculative." From the very first page, Graham distinguishes between investment and speculation. Then at the end of the book, he sums up his advice this way: "Investment is most intelligent when it is most *businesslike* [italics added]. It is amazing to see how many capable businessmen try to operate in Wall Street with complete disregard of all the sound principles through which they have gained success in their own undertakings."

Graham drew a bright line separating investment from speculation and even gambling; a similar demarcation is needed between giving and waste. Too many people giving to important humanitarian causes are, in fact, like the supposed investor who enthusiastically puts good money into bad investments. The difference between success and failure in both investing and giving is the right analysis. Most giving is done speculatively, although we prefer to use softer words such as *hope*, as in, "I hope this will do some good." Instead of guessing or hoping when you give, you can, and should, have confidence in the results of your gift. Just as Benjamin Graham wrote a philosophy for "intelligent investing," this chapter is a parallel philosophy for "intelligent giving."

A $900 Billion Black Hole

I do not believe I am exaggerating by calling the U.S. nonprofit sector "a $900 billion black hole." A similar critique applies worldwide. While the global nonprofit sector is massive, there are few reliable statistics about it. Certainly, donations given through nonprofit groups save lives, make difficult experiences more bearable, provide scholarships, protect the environment, and accomplish other worthy goals every day. Still, the system continues to suck in more resources, while it remains unclear which parts are working well and which are failing. Charities rarely provide meaningful and transparent financial analysis or clear accountability for results. People continue to throw money at problems when there are little or no lasting improvements. Ample research shows that the giving public intuitively senses something is amiss. Surveys regularly report strong misgivings about the results of charity donations, though most people have few ideas for improving them. A Harris Interactive DonorPulse survey released in 2006 found that one-third of U.S. adults think the nonprofit sector is going in a seriously wrong direction. New York University's Wagner Graduate School of Public Service uncovered similar feelings with its polls. NYU's research found that between 30 and 40% of those polled in recent years have only weak levels of confidence in charities. Even among those interviewed who responded positively, researchers found what they called a "glaring weakness." In their words, "81% of the Americans with a great deal of confidence in charitable organizations said charities do only a somewhat good job or worse at spending money wisely."

The United States alone has nearly 2 million registered nonprofit organizations, twice as many as 25 years ago. During the past decade, the number of nonprofit organizations grew nearly three times faster than the number of for-profit businesses. By the time you put together all of the donations, dues, fees, and government grants, the total budget for U.S. nonprofits tops $900 billion a year. These nonprofit groups employ more people than the real estate, insurance, and finance industries combined. Nine out of ten U.S. households give to charitable causes. Is there any other financial sector so large and so important that receives so little scrutiny from its investors?

Where could such reform come from? One possibility is government. In August 2006, a new federal law took effect to end abuses by car donation programs and credit counseling schemes. This reform has been widely hailed and is a good start, but it barely begins to address the overall lack of transparency within the nonprofit sector. More specific evaluation of nonprofit organizations and their work is needed, but is increased federal regulation the solution? A free society benefits from a free charitable sector. So how can we have the best of both worlds: a free charitable sector along with quantifiably great results? The answer lies with donors. Vote with your pocketbook by rewarding groups that accomplish their mission. The most constructive force in philanthropy is intelligent donors. When you give carefully, not only do you help a good cause, but you also encourage progress and accountability among charities.

A common first reaction from people when I talk about accountability is to think I am referring to rooting out corruption. Having managed hundreds of grants, I have discovered that theft is not the biggest problem in the nonprofit sector. The biggest problem is lack of meaningful results. Look at it this way: if you give $10,000 to a cause and nothing changes, you have wasted your money, haven't you? Even if an organization can provide detailed receipts for all expenditures, when the results are minor, your investment was a failure. The word *accountability* sounds similar to the word *accounting*, but in the philanthropic world it must have a broader meaning. Honesty and clean fiduciary practices are necessary, but an organization can be both scrupulous and ineffective. A good habit to develop is to think "accountable *for results*" every time a charity representative or publication says "accountable."

Measuring results makes common sense, but it is not common practice. An extensive study funded by the David and Lucile Packard Foundation examined media coverage of philanthropy between 1990 and 2004. Out of 38,000 stories reviewed on the subject of giving by foundations, only 1% mentioned results from the donations. The study concluded, "Expressions of the benefit or impact of the funding from foundation philanthropy are barely visible among news stories about philanthropy over the last 15 years."

Once again, look at the parallels between investing and philanthropy. Would you pick investments according to the same methods you use to decide your donations? Would you invest in corporations because they *need* your money? Some of the largest automakers in the world need investment right now. Does that make you want to buy their stock? Wise investors typically look for companies on the rise and shun those in trouble. Have you ever noticed how many people do exactly the opposite with charitable giving? They give because they want to help an organization that is struggling financially.

Intelligent givers, by contrast, favor organizations that produce real results.

It is also tempting to give to groups because they focus on people whose situations are heart rending. Fundraisers use powerful and emotional arguments for what sound like worthwhile activities. Always keep in mind, however, that activities are nothing more than the means to an end. Concentrate not on the means but on the results you seek. Do not be distracted by activities or urgency. The seemingly obvious response may in fact be the worst way to help. Consider this all-too-common situation. When famine strikes, sympathetic countries and organizations ship food to keep people alive, but over and over this response backfires.

For instance, in Africa a famine often follows a natural disaster or armed conflict. A consequence of these two situations is that local farmers may be able to produce only half the food people need. So foreign aid organizations ship in free food. That seems humanitarian and logical, right? But even though this solution provides people with enough food in the short term, what happens the following year? Those farmers struggling with poor crops during the crisis are driven completely out of business because, when free food arrives, no one will buy what little the local farmers could produce. This causes an unintended consequence: the program to feed hungry people ends up perpetuating hunger. A more intelligent alternative would be for a humanitarian organization to purchase all the food local farmers produce, but are not able to sell, and assist them in producing more food. Then, if a gap still exists between local supply and local need, ship in additional food. Ideally, food imported should come from neighboring countries, so growing capacity is encouraged in the region. Most food aid today, however, is shipped from halfway around the world. It takes months to arrive and costs usually 50% more than food raised and purchased locally. The result: Africa's hunger problem is worse than ever. One-third of the continent's inhabitants are undernourished, and almost one-quarter of all African children's growth is stunted physically and mentally from malnutrition. Strong evidence suggests that the terms of the aid have compounded the problem. In the world of philanthropy, as in the business world, the terms are critical to the success of the transaction.

Orphans may also suffer from misguided attempts to alleviate their suffering. Orphans and vulnerable children, whom development experts call *OVCs*, are one of the great moral calamities of our time. When we hear about massive numbers of children orphaned by AIDS or by a natural disaster such as a tsunami, it is easy to conclude that orphanages are the answer. This is an example of focusing on activity rather than result. Best practices established by leading groups that work with children in crisis show that the greatest needs of the children are emotional. They need to be bonded long term with a caring family rather than assigned a place in an institution. Programs that enable local families to take in orphans are much better, cheaper, and more scalable solutions than building and maintaining orphanages.

Responsible charities are eager to restore and maintain public trust. As donors, you and I can help that occur by following sound giving practices. Invest your giving so that it actually changes lives for the better. Results count most. Businesslike analysis will make you an intelligent giver. The analysis does not have to be complicated. Simply follow these three rules:

- Have a bottom line
- Measure success
- Support what works

Have a Bottom Line

Intelligent givers always have a bottom line—the outcome they expect from their giving—which can be general or specific. For several years, I managed philanthropy on behalf of an extremely wealthy European family. The bottom line was simply to make sure that lives were being changed as a result of the family's giving. For each donation, I was able to show exactly what kind of changes would result and how many people would benefit. We found outstanding projects to support all over the world.

Your giving becomes an investment when you ask critical questions about outcomes. If your concern is poor children who give up and drop out of school, you may be attracted to tutoring programs; these could be excellent interventions, but only if the organizations measure what, if any, increases occur in the number of children who finish school as a result of the programs. A tutoring program that solicits your money may or may not be effective, which is why it's important to always look at the end result. Stephen Covey in his famous book, *The 7 Habits of Highly Effective People*, advises readers to always, "Begin with the end in mind." Do that with your giving. Decide first what you want to accomplish, and you will make much better decisions about where and how to give based on how well the "end" is being achieved by a particular organization.

Consider a cause like the fight against cancer. I know, personally, just how devastating cancer is. My wife has had three occurrences of cancer over the past three years, involving extensive surgery and months of recuperation. There is no way I would question any of the research leading to her current good health. But even in my gratitude, we are thoughtful about how we give to the fight against cancer.

Don Listwin felt the same way. In 2001, during his tenure as the top executive at the cutting-edge technology firm Cisco Systems, his mother died of ovarian cancer. Determined to make a difference in the ongoing fight against this disease, he became deeply committed to reducing the number of people who die of cancer in the United States each year.

He might have given his money to generic cancer research. But he was disciplined, by his occupation, to look for strategic opportunities. So, instead, he studied cancer, reflected on it, and concluded that early detection currently improves cancer survival rates better than any other intervention. He also saw that most financial support goes to research for treating people already suffering from the disease. Listwin was determined to change that imbalance and has given and raised millions of dollars to target and expand early detection programs.

A safe assumption is that if you're reading this book, you probably want to make a difference. Why else would you give away your money? Think about what kind of a difference you want to make. Who specifically do you want to help? Envision those people. If you are successful with your giving, how will their lives be different? Answering those few questions will provide a point of reference to evaluate your giving options.

Measure Success

Since its early days, the Gates Foundation has aimed to connect the founders' personal desires and values to goals which would shape the foundation's donations and initiatives. These are described on its Web site as follows: "Bill and Melinda Gates believe every life has equal value. In 2000, they created the Bill & Melinda Gates Foundation to help reduce inequities in the United States and around the world."

This description provides important clues specifying the kinds of projects Bill and Melinda Gates intend to support. First, they aim to reduce inequities for people living in the poorest communities compared to the wealthiest. Second, they value every life equally, which is in stark contrast with most giving that stays within a single nation or cultural group. Those two principles provide meaningful guidance about where the foundation will direct its resources. What principles drive your giving? Do you have indicators in mind to assess whether you are getting results that harmonize with your principles? Writing down your objectives in a few succinct sentences, as the Gateses did, will point your giving in the right direction.

After determining what you expect from your giving, the next step is to select one or more indicators of results. For example, you may care especially about children, particularly those who need help most. This sector of philanthropy is also called *children at risk*. After some research, you learn that one subset of the children-at-risk category is street children. Your heart goes out to abandoned youngsters who try to survive without a home or the protection of a caring adult, and your mind then supports your heart's desire, leading you to consider which of those millions of desperate street children you will help. Your mind should also prompt you to comparison-shop among groups that work with street children.

As you think about children at risk, you might begin looking at children in other countries. Right away two regions might come to mind. In Africa, millions of children are orphaned as their parents and other family members have died from AIDS. In Central and South America, according to UNICEF, as many as 40 million children live on the streets. Daily life is brutal; they face crime, violence, drug abuse, and sexual exploitation. The BBC and other reputable news organizations have documented thousands of cases of children being shot to death execution style by the Brazilian police. Hearing these dreadful facts, you might think, "I want to do something about that. I will give some money."

Knowing whom you want to help is an excellent starting point for intelligent giving. Next, investigate what kinds of results are possible when you give money to a program for street children in a place like Brazil. Here's a real life example. For approximately $40,000, a program for children at risk in southeast Brazil expanded with these results:

- More than 100 children rescued from violent households
- 400 children assisted in reporting abuse to authorities they feared
- More than 400 adults recruited to become volunteer agents to protect children
- More than 1,000 children taught how to avoid danger
- Nearly 900 adult family members counseled about child protection

Unfortunately, there is a lot of distraction and even misinformation from charities which obscure your ability to measure results. Charities have become skilled at concealing information they don't want scrutinized. Most understate their actual overhead costs, since many donors ask only superficial questions about fundraising expenses when deciding where to send their money. This has led to the implausible situation, documented by the Center on Philanthropy at Indiana University, in which 37% of U.S. charities claim they spend nothing on fundraising. Nonprofits also have become adept at reclassifying expenses on their financial statements from overhead to appear as program services so as to seem more efficient than they actually are.

Fundraising campaigns use slogans such as, "It only costs $10 to provide a blanket for a disaster victim." That may be the price the charity pays for a blanket, but it does not mean that for every $100 you contribute, 10 more people will have blankets. You want to be an intelligent giver, but how can you gather enough reliable data to do meaningful analysis? There is a simple ratio you can use in almost every giving situation to cut through misinformation or lack of information. Just as price-to-earnings (PE) has become a standard ratio for evaluating investments, there is also a ratio you can use in your philanthropy. It answers the question, "What is the cost of improving one person's life?" I call it the cost-per-life, or CPL, ratio. Using the example of street children in Brazil, that grant had a CPL of only a little over $14. Look at the list of people affected; it totals 2,800 children and adults. Dividing 2,800 into the budget of $40,000 gives you the cost, on average, to change a life in that program.

THE COOL PLACE TO BE

Philanthropy is a growing interest among the more than 8 million Americans whose net worth is greater than $1 million. One indicator of this is the growth in the number of family foundations, up 60% in the past six years. An article in the Work & Money section of the *Christian Science Monitor* said, "Making a global difference is becoming 'the cool place to be' for these wealthy donors." The paper reported, however, that the attraction to international giving is muted by a pair of concerns. "According to Charles Maclean of Philanthropy Now, who did the survey, the rich don't donate for two main reasons: the fear of not having enough money for themselves and their family, and distrust of non-profits. Only 35% said they felt charities would use the money wisely, pointing to a need for objective data on nonprofits."

One well-known charity received more than $300 million in donations for reconstruction following the 2004 Asian tsunami. The charity's main accomplishment was building approximately 5,000 houses. You can easily divide one figure into the other and learn that the cost per house was close to $60,000. By contrast, other organizations in the region that received grants I managed on behalf of donors built homes that ranged in cost between $4,000 and $10,000 per house. If you use CPL, you do not have to personally wade through all the program plans and financial statements of a charity to make a good giving decision. Whether you plan to give $50,000 or $1 million, find out how many lives your contribution will directly affect. Press for a simple, specific list of how many people will be leading better lives and in what ways as a result of your donation. Then you can easily do the math. Divide those results into the amount of your gift. Are you getting good value? By measuring results that are a direct consequence of your donation, not the charity's overall budget, you have a much better idea of the effects of your giving.

Support What Works

When I speak with people about intelligent giving, the principles of having a bottom line and measuring results quickly resonate. The sticking point comes with putting them into practice. Once you determine the outcomes you expect and calculate the real cost of getting those results, the question remains: "How do I go about finding the best groups to support?"

Your best giving will probably be proactive rather than reactive. Here again the contrast is glaring between the way most people invest compared to the way they give. When hurricanes swept through the southern part of the United States in 2005, the lion's share of donations went to the American Red Cross, despite a string of recent controversies within the organization. A *New York Times* editorial on Katrina contributions noted that of $2.7 billion given, more than $1.5 billion went to the American Red Cross. The point here is not to disparage the American Red Cross. Rather, it underscores the fact that many people are likely not aware of the different options available for giving. In the early weeks following Hurricane Katrina, Baptist churches in Texas and other southern states banded together to provide more than 7 million meals. African-American churches were often at the forefront in helping Louisiana residents get settled into new communities. Those groups were far more accountable and delivered a better CPL, making the money donated to these groups more effective than contributions to a huge common pot at a big name charity. Support what works rather than a familiar brand.

Have you ever wondered whether you need to support humanitarian programs in foreign countries when foreign aid is so huge? A common misconception is that governmental foreign aid is so big and run by such competent experts that private donations are not required to address need outside one's own borders. In fact, a closer look reveals that private donations, though much smaller amounts than what is given by governments, often accomplish far more. Since World War II, development aid from governments all over the world to poorer countries totaled $2.5 trillion. George C. Lodge, a member of the Harvard Business School faculty since 1963, has said, "Much of the money goes to governments. The problem is that in many countries of the world, governments lack either the desire or the ability to reduce poverty." That is actually an understatement, because, in many places, living conditions continue to deteriorate despite all the foreign aid received. The British group Oxfam states that food emergencies in Africa occur three times more often today than 20 years ago.

The amounts sent by governments as foreign assistance are so huge that they are difficult to comprehend. Who can wrap their mind around $2.5 trillion? Try this for comparison. Every year *Forbes* magazine produces its list of the 400 richest

Americans. Currently this list includes Bill Gates, Warren Buffett, the Wal-Mart heirs, the founders of Google, and 390 other billionaires. In 2006, for the first time, everyone on the *Forbes* list had net worth above $1 billion. The combined wealth of these top 400 totals approximately $1.25 trillion. Double that, and you have the amount spent on international aid over the last 50 years. If traditional approaches to foreign assistance worked, wouldn't the world be in better shape?

Someone who knows this record well is William Easterly, an economist who spent 16 years working at the World Bank. His book, *The White Man's Burden*, describes aid history in detail. Far from being all doom and gloom, he sets out a key principle for obtaining positive results. In the first chapter, he draws a distinction between *searchers* and *planners*. His contrast is akin to the difference I have seen between top-down and bottom-up approaches to meeting human needs. The top-down mentality says that experts, whether government technocrats, academics, or career development staff, know what is best. They devise brilliant plans, and if people in developing countries would just follow those plans, everything would get better. Planners have a long, sad history of great ideas that fail when implemented.

For example, lately I have been hearing a lot about fantastic new technologies to provide clean water in places where there is extensive waterborne disease. But should we be dispensing expensive, high-tech solutions before we have taken advantage of all the cheap, yet effective low-tech options available? I have found that even the poorest people on earth are inventive and industrious. Given the slightest assistance in support of their plans, they will achieve lasting results at very low cost. I recall being in West Africa during the hottest season and visiting a new well that villagers had dug by hand. All they needed to complete their water system was some concrete to shore up the walls along with plastic pipe and a hand pump to extract the water. This is what Easterly calls the *searcher* approach. He puts it this way, "A Searcher hopes to find answers to individual problems only by trial and error experimentation. A Planner believes outsiders know enough to impose solutions. A Searcher believes only insiders have enough knowledge to find solutions, and that most solutions must be homegrown."

AS SEEN ON TV

Most people in the West admit to conflicted feelings when they see images of starving people on television and in print. They recoil at the dying babies, distended bellies, and tattered clothes, yet feel pressured by guilt to donate.

These photos have sparked vigorous discussion among charity professionals, some of whom have coined the term *development pornography*. Such campaigns, they assert, stereotype the developing world as uniformly inferior to the West, dehumanize the suffering people portrayed, and mask the issues underlying poverty which include public health, corruption, and gender discrimination.

Fortunately, this skewed view of the developing world is not the whole story. There are millions of impoverished people who are capable and eagerly awaiting a chance to work their way out of poverty through the interventions described in this book.

Resist being enticed to donate because of clever new ideas, convincing presentations, or winsome fundraisers. A more intelligent way to give is to find a group that has a proven track record and back it in a way that allows the group to take the same benefits to more people. The process of identifying excellent projects to support has not been difficult for me. In every corner of the globe, I have found scrappy local groups deeply dedicated to their communities. In many cases, they have delivered successful projects that have rescued children, or provided clean water, or some other major lifesaving accomplishment with little or no money. Getting behind these unsung heroes and providing the funds to double or triple their impact is an exceptional way to achieve your philanthropic objectives. An added benefit is that the cost to change a life is minimal.

Having worked with microcredit programs for years, I have noticed that donors to these types of programs seem to have a remarkably high level of satisfaction. The reason may be that most microcredit programs easily pass all three tests for intelligent giving. The results of programs that provide loans to poor entrepreneurs are clear and measurable. As poor families cease being poor, they move out of deprivation. In our world where so many are trapped in a downward spiral, microcredit reverses the trend into an upward spiral.

" *The poor stay poor not because they are lazy,*
but because they have no access to capital. "

—MILTON FRIEDMAN,
1976 NOBEL PRIZE IN ECONOMIC SCIENCES

CHAPTER 3

GIVING CREDIT WHERE CREDIT IS DUE

Phil Smith

M y break came from a $50,000 loan and the opportunity to invest in a new gas pipeline company. Eric's big opportunity came when he lined up financing to grow his television production business in Chicago. A microcredit loan is often the only break impoverished people receive that can move them up the rungs of the economic ladder in their communities.

The fundamental premise of microcredit is that people can improve their incomes through hard work if given small loans to strengthen their businesses. This premise has been proven true by millions of borrowers who are now building their tiny businesses, supporting their families, and repaying their microloans so that others can have a chance at the one break they too need to succeed. These borrowers are actively changing the futures of their families instead of begging or help-lessly waiting for the next installment of charity aid, which may never come.

Sam Daley-Harris, director of the Microcredit Summit Campaign, reports in *The State of the Microcredit Summit Campaign Report 2006* that in the fall of 2006, 3,133 microfinance institutions served 113 million families during the previous year. While that is a laudable accomplishment, more than 500 million families that would almost certainly benefit from microcredit remain impoverished, and at least another 300 million more might benefit from it. According to our best calculations, Eric and I estimate that only one out of every eight people who could benefit from microcredit currently has access to it. This is very clearly an underserved market.

As a weapon against poverty in developing countries, microcredit is as vital as education, health, human rights, and good government. To highlight its importance in eliminating poverty, the United Nations declared 2005 the International Year of Microcredit. Richard Weingarten, executive secretary of the U.N. Capital Development Fund, said, "The demand for microfinance services remains largely unmet, especially in Africa." Despite this, less than 1% of World Bank funding goes to microcredit.

So, why does microcredit work so well in developing countries? The answer is so subtle that despite having read extensively about microcredit, I still missed the underlying and seldom discussed reason: the economies of developing countries are entirely different from those of developed countries. These economies operate on a much smaller scale, a micro-scale, compared to the economies of the developed world. This distinction is important because virtually all of the people who live in abject poverty live in developing countries or in the undeveloped regions of partially developed countries, such as India and China. The income and expenses of these people represent but a tiny fraction of the same amount in developed nations, and they make their livings in ways bearing little resemblance to those seen in the developed world. What you and I might consider pocket change can represent a doubling of income for impoverished people.

MICROCREDIT   IN ACTION

The Mikhayloynas were struggling in Ukraine. They were living in an unheated, half-built house that they could not afford to finish, and their government pension barely covered the cost of their food. With no money for medicine or other necessities, Galina Mikhayloyna started selling milk in jars at the local outdoor market where vendors sell everything from hand-knit socks to home-baked bread. She soon was able to add grain to her merchandise, but did not have enough money to build up her supply or to stock other products. Galina obtained a $400 microloan which she used to increase and diversify her inventory with a variety of popular household products. Sale of these additional products produced enough extra income for the Mikhayloynas to be able to finish their house. Subsequent loans helped Galina move up to the best selling place in the market. She now has many customers and is known throughout the market as a strong businesswoman and savvy entrepreneur.

Cash Only

What may at first appear to tourists as a flea market when visiting a developing country is in fact the community's version of a town mega-mall where, instead of the credit and debit transactions we in the developed world are used to, all exchanges of goods are in cash. In the place of mass-produced name-brand groceries and dry goods, the market sells homegrown produce, household goods in small quantities, such as single bars of soap or a few squares of toilet paper, and clothing—much of it locally produced—plus a very limited assortment of small luxuries that only a few shoppers can afford. The local equivalent of a surround sound widescreen movie complex is a battered television propped up on the back of a rusty pickup truck. The market's gourmet store equivalent is a gravity-defying basket on a woman's head from which she sells fruit otherwise unavailable in her village. These vendors work hard to provide for their families. Many work from dawn to dusk for incomes that, without a little credit, often do not meet their families' basic needs.

Imagine living in a society where every financial transaction had to be completed in cash, a society with no banks or alternative sources for loans and with no other access to financial services. You could not write a check or charge a purchase. Your savings account would be cash under the mattress or in your pocket. Accumulating enough cash to make a major purchase such as a car or a house would be nearly impossible. Investing would be too cumbersome to imagine, so there would be no stock market; companies that require investment capital to start up would never get off the ground. You would find it difficult to expand sales for your tiny enterprise, because your inventory of clothes, produce, or basic household items would be limited to what your meager profit would buy. You could not borrow to buy, repair, or replace equipment, and, since you have no reserves, small emergencies would turn into disasters. Yet more than half the world's population operates in this type of cash-only, informal economy.

In contrast, intricate banking and finance systems fuel developed countries' economies by providing loans and other financial services for creditworthy customers and working capital for potentially profitable businesses. In contrast with a cash-only economy, developed countries are moving toward a cashless society.

In developing countries, government regulations, when they exist, often obstruct rather than support business. Laws, when enforced, are complex and regressive. They seldom protect individual property rights. Virtually no formal banking or financing services are available except for wealthy clients in the big cities. Few salaried or full-time hourly jobs exist. *The Economist* reported that nearly 60% of nonagricultural employment in Latin America and 67% in Africa is in the informal sector. In India, nine out of ten workers are in the informal sector, contributing 60% of net domestic product and 70% of income. Informal businesses are typically the only viable employment options for the poor. The one positive aspect of this type of business is that all workers can be self-employed provided they are smart enough, work hard, have inventory and a market, and keep their prices competitive.

In developing countries, most poor people do not have access to financial services. Either credit is not available from any source or only from unscrupulous lenders. Their interest demands are so exorbitant that no matter how good the business and no matter how hardworking the entrepreneur, it is impossible to get ahead. Citigroup, the largest banking network in the world, is beginning to look seriously at ways to connect with the vast numbers of people who live completely outside banking as it exists today. Robert Annibale directs the Citigroup division studying microcredit. He points out that 2.5 billion people have never used a bank or, as he put it, "40% of the world is beyond the world we know." Yet, with just a tiny amount of fair credit, people are able to open and expand businesses by adding inventory or equipment, implementing a competitive advantage, or seizing a market opportunity.

MICROCREDIT   IN ACTION

Like many women in southern Haiti, Marie Laursa had a family to support but no money and little education. With cash in hand from a microloan, she acquired the bargaining power to purchase rice from nearby farmers at the best possible price. She took that rice to the city where she now had the staying power to command a good price for it. She promptly took the proceeds from that sale and bought consumer goods to sell in her village. With her new export/import business, she is able to send her daughter to school and break the cycle of poverty into which she was born.

Though the income derived from microbusinesses is not large, neither is the cost of living of the individuals who run them. That is why the minor increase in income, which stems from appropriate use of microcredit, can give families the financial boost necessary to increase their standard of living.

With subsequent larger loans, businesses can grow and move these families even further up the economic ladder. This is real progress, perhaps the first progress some families have seen in generations. Working with passion, parents are ensuring that their children will not suffer as they have. For this privilege they readily sign their names on the legal papers for microloans and work hard to reimburse their lenders.

Microenterprises

Microenterprises are small-scale versions of the same types of businesses found in developed countries. Twenty hens and a coop constructed from scrap material become a poultry enterprise. A produce store may be a rickety wooden cart piled with mangos picked that morning by the driver or purchased from a local farmer. Hives, bees, and a collection of mismatched used jars are a honey factory. A 40-year-old truck is used to transport both goods for sale and paying passengers. A pedal-powered sewing machine is the local equivalent of a clothing factory. An outdoor clay oven is the village bakery. With a microloan providing working capital, these businesses can support families and boost the grassroots economy for the whole community.

Being creative and turning every available resource into a business is vital to improving the lives of those in poverty. In the Caribbean, a young man used a microloan to buy a used TV and VCR. He has turned his two-room tenement apartment into a movie theater. He rents a new video every day, charges neighbors the equivalent of 15 cents to watch the movie, and sells snacks from his four-shelf grocery store. In Asian villages with no electricity, "phone ladies" buy cell phones with microloans and make their livelihoods by serving as their villages' pay telephones. A man in India with a laundry business was not making enough money to survive. Washing his customers' clothes in a nearby stream was not the problem; giving them a fresh-pressed appearance afterward was. A microloan of $50 was all he needed to acquire an iron and an electrical outlet, bringing his business to the next level.

Poor people often do not need outsiders to tell them about business opportunities. They are keenly aware of opportunities to start or grow a microenterprise. Usually they just need a little working capital. As I got involved in microcredit, two factors became blatantly obvious. First, I was so used to living in a society awash with capital that I had a hard time conceiving of a world where absolutely no borrowed funds were available. Second, most poor people in developing countries are intelligent and hard-working. They know that if they do not work, their families do not eat.

One of the first stories I heard about microcredit revealed the way families and societies can blossom on a lasting basis when offered the opportunity. Years ago in a shantytown in Managua, Nicaragua, before the opening of a community microcredit bank, all the homes were made of scrap wood, plastic sheeting, and cardboard, and the local schoolteacher lamented that too many youngsters were working or begging instead of attending school. At an orientation meeting to introduce the concept of a microcredit bank, few residents took an active interest in the proposal. The people of this community had given up all hope of changing their situation.

In that same neighborhood, two years after the program opened, cement block houses stood among the shanties, and the community's teacher was excited because more children were attending school. The borrowers were proud of their businesses and home improvements. One weekly meeting was lively, as the members celebrated their successful lobbying of government officials to have electricity brought to their area. Some borrowers volunteered to dig holes for the utility poles, and others offered to provide refreshments. They concluded their time together with a discussion of how electricity would improve their businesses. One woman planned to use her next loan to buy a refrigerator so she could sell milk and meat in addition to bread and soap. A carpenter predicted that he could more than double his production with a power saw.

Instead of resigning themselves to remaining poor and being fearful of sliding deeper into poverty, these successful borrowers made the decision to improve their lives. Before they experienced the power of credit, the people of this Managua shantytown would not have dared to approach a government official for the electrical service they needed and were entitled to receive. The villagers would not have dug holes for utility poles, because they would not have believed poles would arrive. Nor would they have planned refreshments for the volunteer diggers, because they would not have had enough food.

Over a two-year span, the people in that microcredit program in Nicaragua made the mental move into the middle class. They still did not have running water, and most of their floors remained nothing but packed dirt. When they had transportation, it was usually a donkey. But the progress is unmistakable. In the past, the next generation had no reason to expect they could improve on their parents' lot in life. Now most of the children receive an elementary education, which is a solid middle-class achievement by local standards.

MICROCREDIT   IN ACTION

Peter Greer, who built the largest microcredit program in Rwanda, now heads microcredit programs in a dozen countries. When I asked him to recount his most vivid memory of a borrower helped by one of his programs, he told me, "I will never forget Mama Ndugu. She received a small loan to set up a grocery shop on her porch and in her house. She also farmed land behind her home when the shop was closed. Her business was prospering, and she told me how she was now able to provide for her children and several orphans she had taken in. Despite her humble surroundings, she was proud to be caring properly for her family. As I was about to leave, she presented me with a giant yam, the best from her garden. I had given her nothing other than a loan, which she paid in full and on time. She is the one who gave something to me—not just a yam, but a new appreciation of the generosity and dignity that make the poor rich."

Success Is Changed Lives

In *The World Is Flat*, Thomas L. Friedman observes that when people have hope, they are in the middle class. "They have a pathway out of poverty or lower-income status toward a higher standard of living and a better future for their kids. You can be middle class in your head whether you make $2 a day or $200, if you believe in social mobility—that your kids have a chance to live better than you do—and that hard work and playing by the rules of your society will get you where you want to go."

While receiving a yam as a hospitality gift may seem incidental to us, in the context of the poverty of the developing world it represents an enormous generosity that is humbling to experience. For people who have long lived without enough to eat, the opportunity to show their gratitude with such a small gift represents considerable progress. Some of the most crucial benefits of microcredit are far more than financial and cannot be measured on a balance sheet. The true benefits are dignity and self-esteem, along with respect for family and community. Microcredit enables people to become givers, not takers. Microcredit should not be seen as charity but rather as the opportunity poor people need to build a decent life. Through microcredit, donors can shed the old hand-out mentality and become true partners in progress with the people of the developing world.

> *" Money is the seed of money,*
> *and the first guinea is sometimes more difficult*
> *to acquire than the second million. "*
> —JEAN-JACQUES ROUSSEAU

CHAPTER 4

BAREFOOT BANKING

Eric Thurman

When Mao Zedong came to power in China, healthcare for the masses was one of his most daunting challenges. One child in five died in infancy. Overall life expectancy was only 35 years. China was pegged with the unflattering nickname "the sick man of Asia." Peasant farmers, who made up most of the population, rarely had access to medical services of any kind.

While Mao's programs such as the Great Leap Forward and the Cultural Revolution are broadly criticized, his program for public health remains a legend. In 1978, a conference of the World Health Organization unanimously passed the Declaration of Alma-Ata praising the Chinese solution for universal healthcare, a solution that became known as *barefoot doctors*.

In 1965 Chairman Mao announced his plan to provide healthcare services to rural China using barefoot doctors. They were simply farmers from different agricultural communes who had received a few months of practical medical training. They learned to dispense drugs, set bones, deliver babies, and treat wounds and many common diseases. Returning to their homes after the training, they split their time between farming and treating fellow workers. This program brought at least a rudimentary level of healthcare to all levels of society. The British Institute for Development Studies at the University of Sussex in Brighton spoke highly of the barefoot doctors program in its July 1995 policy briefing, *Paying for Health—New Lessons from China*: "By the end of the 1970s, China had a very effective rural health service. . . . Approximately 85% of villages had a health station staffed by one or more primary health care workers, known as 'barefoot doctors.' They ensured that most of the population received treatment for illness, and help and advice on how to prevent disease." At its peak, the corps of barefoot doctors totaled more than 1 million peasant paramedics. This collective approach to medical care collapsed in 1981 concurrent with the end of agricultural communes.

During the nearly three decades that barefoot doctors were on the front line of Chinese medicine, the data show that they measurably improved the health of the nation. The Harvard School of Public Health wrote about these improvements in the summer 2006 edition of the *Harvard Public Health Review*: "Mao's emphasis on public health enabled China to curb rampant diseases, from polio and smallpox to diarrhea and schistosomiasis. The barefoot doctors dug millions of latrines to make water supplies safer, taught people to prepare foods hygienically, and administered vaccines. Between 1952 and 1985, China's average life expectancy rose from 35 to 68 years. Infant mortality plummeted from 200 deaths per 1,000 live births to 40."

Just as barefoot doctors were vital to bringing basic health-care to previously underserved populations in China, a similar approach is now required to address the absence of legitimate financial services for the majority of the world's people. In a parallel to China's barefoot doctors program, microcredit is sometimes referred to as *barefoot banking*.

Barefoot doctors were never meant to conjure up the image of their big city counterparts, in crisp white uniforms working in clean, modern hospitals. Likewise, microcredit officers are in stark contrast to the image of bankers in the developed world. Visiting a local microcredit office, you should expect to see the staff in casual street clothes instead of three-piece Savile Row suits and Hermès neckties. In the place of polished marble counters, carpets, and luxury cars parked in reserved spaces, you are more likely to find a rusty bicycle or motor scooter leaning against a tree outside a small, sparsely fur-nished office.

Barefoot banking may sound quaint, but do not underesti-mate its importance or power. Microcredit has an impressive record of changing lives. Keep in mind, however, that author-ity in microcredit rests more with members of the borrowers group than with the loan officers. Peer pressure within groups of borrowers guarantees that everyone pays on time. All finan-cial transactions take place in the open at regular group meet-ings. This approach ensures mutual accountability and builds trust quickly in communities where corruption and exploita-tion have long been the norm.

These grassroots financial institutions are generally referred to as *community* or *village banks*. The following story, a composite of many similar stories, gives a hypothetical example of how a typical community bank works.

I Trust You

A nonprofit microcredit organization based in Tegucigalpa, Honduras, raised $25,000 from U.S. contributors with a plan to open several more community bank branches in remote villages of Honduras. One of its loan officers, who managed other branches in the region, rode his motorbike to one of these villages and invited residents to the local school to hear about a new way to improve their lives. The people, who were naturally skeptical about this sort of offer, learned he was from a neighboring village, and so agreed to listen to what he had to say.

Roberto, a *vulcanizadoro*, or tire repairman, was incredulous that a bank would travel to his village. The only banks he knew of were two hours away in Tegucigalpa, the capital, and no one he knew had ever crossed their guarded thresholds. He knew that the poor—people like him—were not potential bank customers. His wife, Elisa, was excited about what this new local bank might mean for them, but he tried to dispel what he considered her silly notions that any bank would actually help them. He went to the meeting anticipating disappointment. He was born poor, and he expected to die poor.

Roberto's first surprise was the banker who greeted him at the door. He was Bernardo Estaban. Roberto had patched a tire for him several months earlier. Bernardo was one of the fortunate few from their region who had gone to high school in Tegucigalpa. Shortly after the meeting began, Roberto realized that Bernardo was working to find ways to make loans, not excuses to refuse them. During the meeting, Roberto learned that people who received loans would meet weekly to get to know one another and to learn basic business practices and how to use credit responsibly. Participants would join a group of eight borrowers who cross-guarantee one another's loans. In addition, their initial group of eight would cross-guarantee the loans of two other eight-member lending groups. The groups would continue to meet every week until all their loans were fully repaid. Roberto realized they would probably want to stay together even longer, because once their loans were paid back they could qualify for larger loans.

Following the meeting, Bernardo shook Roberto's hand and said something Roberto never expected to hear. "I know you will pay us back. I trust you and your friends." Roberto rushed home to tell Elisa. She was not sure they should trust some of the men, but Roberto assured her that he and the other men would keep pressure on everyone to honor their agreements with the bank and with one another. They discussed how a $200 microloan would buy needed inventory and tools for Roberto's tire business. In the past, he had missed chances to make money because he did not have the tools and spare parts required to help people who needed specialty tires repaired or replaced. They penciled some numbers on scrap paper and did the math. After repaying two $200 microloans, Roberto should be able to double the sales of his tiny business. Better than that, his net income would triple.

Within several months Elisa came to appreciate the wisdom of the bank's lending procedures. All 24 men who received loans met faithfully every Tuesday night. For the first time in the history of the village, they gathered to discuss business instead of to drink beer and chat about politics and women. Each man had to make his $10 weekly payment publicly to Bernardo. The rare defaulter had a lot of explaining to do, not just to Bernardo, but to the others who had guaranteed his loan. After completing the payments and recordkeeping, the men energetically discussed their businesses and offered advice to one another. Bernardo presented short training sessions on pertinent topics such as inventory control and price setting. While he made suggestions during the meeting, the borrowers were in charge. Before long they preferred to call themselves members rather than borrowers.

Over time the members came to fully understand the importance of paying back their loans completely and on time. It was the only way they could qualify for additional, larger loans. Their incomes were increasing. They were envisioning new business possibilities in future loans. Now their wives wanted loans, too. The men liked the idea that with microloans their wives could contribute more to each family's economic stability.

The microcredit organization that started the community bank was pleased, but not surprised, to see it thrive. With proof of progress in hand, it was easy to raise additional money from donors to increase the community bank's capitalization to serve even more clients.

The Nuts and Bolts of Community Banking

Barefoot banking may be simple, but it operates according to proven, well-documented principles. The following are a few of the guiding principles that are the norm in the microcredit industry:

- *Small loans* increase borrowers' incomes by allowing them to seize business opportunities or supply day-to-day working capital. Depending on the economic level of the country, initial loans usually range between $50 and $500. Inexperienced microcredit programs tend to lend too much money rather than too little. One of the most important characteristics of a good microcredit organization is having the local knowledge to make loans that are neither too big nor too small.

- *Small groups* of entrepreneurs cross-guarantee one another's loans. This provides a strong incentive to repay. Tight community bonds are forged, and the resulting peer pressure and peer support are more effective than collateral in ensuring loan repayment. Members patronize one another's businesses and work together to ensure that everyone succeeds.
- *Short terms* help people who are new to credit learn how to use it and be responsible. Initial terms of four to six months keep borrowers from becoming complacent and allow the community bank to recycle the money into new loans more often.
- *Frequent payments* create financial discipline and keep the borrowers from falling behind. Considering the economic difficulties of the poor, making weekly payments is much easier than accumulating larger amounts for monthly payments. So, weekly meetings are usually mandatory.
- *Potential future, larger loans* motivate borrowers to pay back their first loans. Graduating up the scale also helps members expand their microbusinesses. It is common to see successful borrowers hire additional workers from their community as their businesses grow.

GRADUATION DAY

A significant motivation for borrowers to repay their loans is to qualify for larger, follow-up loans. Their first loan may be $100, the second $200, the third $400, and the final loan $600. The industry calls this process *graduating*. Eventually, this cycle of borrowing and paying back should end, either because the borrower's business has enough retained earnings to supply its own working capital or because the borrower is now established well enough to transition into the regular banking system.

However, clients may occasionally leave microcredit programs for less positive reasons. The loans fail to help them for some reason, or the organization may conclude it would rather make $100 loans to six different people than one larger loan to a repeat borrower. The worst scenario is when the lending organization simply runs out of money and cannot offer bigger loans.

When an entrepreneur steps out of the revolving loans cycle because her business becomes strong enough to stand on its own, she has graduated from the largest, most difficult school in the world—the University of Poverty.

One worry I hear occasionally from donors just beginning to support microcredit organizations is whether payment collection methods are effective. They are surprised to learn that repayment rates for good microcredit programs typically exceed 98%, primarily because of cross-guarantees and the incentive of additional loans. When it is required, however, microcredit collections are just as effective as traditional collection agencies, only more personal and creative. In Zimbabwe, a debt collection task fell to a loan officer. Since he had grown up in the community, he understood the culture and knew what he needed to do. He called on the borrower in default and visited with her throughout an afternoon. Graciously and at length, he asked about her family, including distant relatives. He talked about the weather and politics, complimented her children, and helped her son with his homework. Finally, to avoid having to invite him to stay for dinner, she paid her debt.

Interest and Fees Make Microcredit Programs Sustainable

In the absence of microcredit, poor people who must borrow money resort to borrowing from loan sharks who inflict crushing interest charges on those who are desperate for a little cash. The abusive 5-6 scheme practiced by unscrupulous lenders in the Philippines is a typical example. A 5 peso loan at dawn requires a 6 peso payback by nightfall. That is 20% interest per day or, assuming a six-day work week, more than 6,000% interest per year! If for any reason a borrower defaults, collection methods can be brutal. In contrast, interest on microloans is much lower, and the penalties for default, while serious, do not involve physical punishment or cruel methods. The greatest consequence of failure to repay a loan is the loss of both respect in the community and the chance for future loans.

Donors new to microcredit may be surprised to discover a program they support is charging up to 50% interest annually. Is this usury? No. My experience is that when microcredit programs err with interest rates, it is not by charging too much, but rather too little, failing to cover the real costs of delivering their services. Closer inspection shows interest rates charged by microcredit providers usually range from about 10 to 15% plus the inflation rate for the country. So the effective interest rate, adjusted for inflation, is quite reasonable. Microcredit organizations must be self-sustaining, able to absorb operating costs, the few bad debts, and currency fluctuations. Otherwise, the only way to cover the shortfall is to take money out of the loan pool. Decapitalizing the loan portfolio will cause the program to stall and eventually fail. In the dozens of countries where I have visited microcredit groups, the unanimous opinion among borrowers is that having loans available at a fair cost is what they want most. Availability of decent loans is far more important to them than shaving a few points off the interest rates. Without microcredit, there is either no other place to borrow or people have to resort to moneylenders who charge abusive rates.

A thorough analysis of what constitutes a fair level of interest is a big enough topic to merit an entire book of its own. Briefly, however, it is generally agreed that the best practices for microcredit banking fly in the face of conventional wisdom. For instance, it is commonly thought that because loan recipients are poor, they should be charged a low interest rate, one that is subsidized below the local market rate. After years of experience, I have learned that programs applying such artificially low rates usually fail because interest discounts are used to prop up weak businesses that should, instead, be allowed to close. What poor people need are authentic, durable sources of income. They should not borrow for their businesses unless the loans, including interest, will have the net result of boosting their income. This has become the guiding principle I use to determine fair interest rates for microloans.

MICROCREDIT   IN ACTION

In Tamil Nadu, the southern-most state in India, Shanti, a 28-year-old mother of two young sons, weaves delicate silk saris to sell in her neighborhood. Born into the extreme poverty rampant in this region, Shanti's weaving skills were hard won, and she has worked diligently since childhood just to survive. Though renowned for the quality of her saris, Shanti was earning only $2.60 per day, barely enough to allow her to care for her children. Desperate for the capital required to expand her business, she became indebted to a local loan shark who charged outrageous interest rates. Later, she learned about microcredit and took a loan for $60 that she invested in her business. Her income has since increased to more than $6 a day, and she is now free from crippling debt. Today, Shanti is able to focus on growing her business and creating a better life for her family.

Stability through Savings

Barefoot banking frequently involves more than loans, just as formal commercial banking does. One additional activity common among microcredit groups is savings. Is it surprising that poor people are avid savers? Outsiders may guess that borrowers are too poor to save, but in fact they are too poor not to save. Savings may take the form of a piglet raised to sell to pay for next year's school fees, or coins accumulated one at a time in a tin box under the bed. Those savings are often the only safety net for the impoverished.

In the developing world, demand is high for savings services. Poor people are looking for someone who will hold and protect the little bit of cash they can gather. An extra animal they have raised, or money they have hidden in their shanty, is not enough and often is not secure. Earning interest on savings deposits, however, is beyond their comprehension. The more common experience of those trying to save in the developing world is to actually receive negative interest on their savings. People who want the safety of keeping their savings at a bank end up paying for that "privilege." Here is how it happens. Someone in the community who has status and sufficient net worth will open a new account at a bank. Doing so puts that person into business as a savings broker. He or she then collects money from many different people and deposits their combined savings into the savings account. The savings broker then keeps all the interest earned and on top of that charges an assistance fee. Although clearly the opposite of what we think of as savings, for thousands upon thousands of poor people, it is their only option. With this arrangement, at least they know their money is secure and available when they need it, assuming the collector is honest, which, sadly, may not always be the case.

Given these difficulties with savings, it is no wonder that the savings services available through community banks can be so important. An added benefit to having one's own saving account is that all account holders actually earn interest on their money. Many microcredit providers require small, regular savings deposits along with weekly loan payments. Such compulsory savings are more than collateral on outstanding loans; they help the poor accumulate useful sums of money for business expansion and family needs, such as a bed, a stove, or school fees. While increasing the economic stability of the borrowers, savings also may supplement the pool of funds available for loans. Not every microcredit program can offer savings, however, depending on a country's banking regulations. Here's where local ingenuity comes into play. To satisfy restrictions preventing community banks from collecting and holding savings directly, some programs combine borrowers' savings into a single bank account held in the name of the microcredit organization. This is an adaptation of the previously described method with the exploitative savings broker. The difference is that the microcredit group works the system for the benefit of the savings group members.

The savings issue has helped fuel a major trend over the past few years of nonprofit microcredit organizations choosing to convert into formal financial institutions with full banking licenses. The process of qualifying for and obtaining banking accreditation is difficult and costly. Nevertheless, more and more microcredit organizations are going that route, which enables them to scale up, serve more people, and offer a broader range of services.

Progress in overcoming regulatory barriers is now happening in two ways. One, just described, has nonprofit microcredit organizations reaching up to meet all the legal and capitalization requirements to become accredited, for-profit banks serving the poor. The other form of progress has governments reaching down from their lofty requirements for banks and embracing microcredit groups, giving them special authority to collect savings and perform other financial services. Both forms of progress should be encouraged.

A Pillar in the Community, but without a Building

Community banks function as banks without walls for the benefit of small groups of borrowers who may meet in a one-room school, someone's shanty home, or literally under a tree. The back office for the lending system may be relatively advanced with computers and Internet access, or it may simply be a stack of paper receipts tabulated meticulously by hand on antiquated adding machines. Tracking individual accounts is not that difficult, but the task becomes complicated when there are thousands of clients making tiny weekly payments, often less than a dollar at a time. All of this requires supervision by trained credit officers who meet regularly with the groups. Typical microcredit workers monitor hundreds of accounts each. Then, at the head office, capable senior managers must maintain up-to-the-minute, accurate summary information to spot and address any problems before they become a firestorm of trouble.

Not many of these bankers for the poor are barefoot any-more, though many of them have nothing more than shoe leather to transport them to borrower meetings. Having spent time with hundreds of these workers over the years, I never cease to be impressed by their dedication, cultural insight, and personal integrity. They do hard work carefully managing what seem like negligible amounts of money, but they have good reason. Those small loans often bring gigantic improvements in the lives of the people who use them.

" Give me a lever long enough and a place to stand, and I can move the world. "

—ARCHIMEDES

CHAPTER 5

MOVING THE WORLD

Phil Smith

In the summer of 1996, Ken Hersh, David Albin, and I cel-ebrated in Ken's corner office. Six years earlier, Ken and David's investment group, Natural Gas Partners, had invested $10 million to bootstrap a small oil company of which I was the CEO. With the other directors, we guided the company through a merger, an IPO, and complex bank loans. This financial engineering, combined with the company's good performance, turned a $10 million stake into a $70 million dream investment. The power of financial leverage trans-formed a good project into a great project, a seven-bagger, a return of seven to one. Even Sir John Templeton would have been proud.

Eight years and several companies later, I met with Ken and David to discuss the idea of using financial engineering with microcredit. They instantly grasped the concept and were astonished at the variety and impact of levers that could be applied to this area of philanthropy. They offered several new financial ideas concerning letters of credit and invited me to make a presentation introducing microcredit to hundreds of guests at their upcoming charity golf tournament.

The thrill of telling the microcredit story to my colleagues left me as weak-kneed as had my four-foot putts earlier that tournament day. The audience members were accustomed to hearing pitches about high-risk investments. Some had spent tens of millions of dollars drilling nine-inch holes several miles into the earth knowing the majority of them would be dry and worthless. They knew the importance of reducing risk and increasing returns. Microcredit immediately captured their imaginations since most of them had borrowed money to start their own businesses. They grasped the importance of microentrepreneurs gaining a competitive advantage through more inventory, better equipment, or lower costs. They understood that business practices are basically the same whether using $50 or $50 million of borrowed capital. In the end, though, the irresistible hook was the ability to leverage philanthropic investments beyond what any of them had ever been able to do in business.

The Currency/Country Lever

The first way to multiply the power of your money is to use it in an underdeveloped country. The poorer the community, the less money it takes to start or improve a microbusiness capable of supporting a family, and the less it costs to live there. Underdeveloped countries have informal economies where self-employed people face little government regulation or other profit barriers. A street vendor selling homemade tortillas does not require a business permit or a building. A home kitchen does not come under public heath department regulations and inspections.

MICROCREDIT IN ACTION

Crucita lives in a batey, a tiny, impoverished village in the Dominican Republic, an hour's drive from the nearest town, Consuelo. Her first microloan purchased additional food and soft drinks for the stand her family runs. After she repaid her first loan, she increased her business activity with five more loans. Now her capital investments include an oven, freezer, washing machine, and a small motorcycle, which have allowed her business to branch out into a bakery, frozen foods store, laundry, and a transportation service. Her son taxis people to town and transports merchandise back to Crucita, making money from each leg of the journey. Some of her best customers are her fellow borrowers from the community bank. They encourage one another, share business tips, and offer help in times of need. They have learned that by working together, all may succeed.

There is no exact formula to determine the total dollar amount in loans it takes to move a family up the poverty ladder. Rather than getting lost in a forest of details, the following rule of thumb works well across a wide spectrum of countries and situations: whether it is in one loan or a series of loans, the total amount of borrowed funds needed to help lift someone from poverty is roughly equal to the average annual income per capita of the borrower's country (which is defined as the World Bank's GNI per capita 2005, Atlas method). Based on this rule, the total amount of loans would be as low as $120 in parts of Africa and as high as $4,460 in Russia. According to this same approximation, to establish or improve a small business that would significantly increase a poor family's standard of living, a hard-working entrepreneur would need to borrow about $43,740 in the United States or £22,650 ($37,600) in the United Kingdom.

Therefore, on a cost basis, the most extraordinary opportunities for changing lives are in the world's poorest countries. With this lever alone, your money in a poor country can be 365 times as powerful as compared to using it in the United States, or 313 times in the United Kingdom!

The Loan Recycling Lever

Virtually all charitable donations run quickly through a charity's fingers to pay for overhead, equipment, buildings, and direct client services. Even when a charity is highly efficient, your donation is rarely used more than once. In contrast, microloans, when properly made, have a typical repayment period of six months or less, and then the money recycles as a new loan. Over the span of a decade, up to 20 microbusinesses are started or strengthened with the amount of just one loan. Therefore, the power of money multiplies approximately 20 times through microcredit compared to one-time charity expenditures.

Multiply the lever of using money in an undeveloped country (up to 365) by the lever of loan recycling (20), and the result is that you are able to exert as much as 7,300 times more power when you provide microloans in a poor country compared to donating to a humanitarian cause in a developed country. And, as late-night television infomercials trumpet, "that's not all." Additional levers can be applied for even larger outcomes.

The Financial Engineering Lever

Instead of operating solely with donations, many microcredit providers also borrow money to make microloans. The following example shows how this can leverage the impact of your giving. A microcredit project in India was financed with great imagination. A donor made a $30,000 contribution and loaned an additional $230,000 to the Grameen Foundation. The foundation and its partner in India used the loan as security to borrow $2.6 million from an Indian financial source. Over four years, the $2.6 million would be used for microloans, and it would be reloaned at least six times for a total of $15.6 million in loans. At the end of four years, the $2.6 million loan would be repaid, and the $230,000 returned to the donor. For a tax-deductible donation of $30,000 and the use of $230,000 for four years, this donor expects to help create or improve businesses for more than 25,000 impoverished families, comprising some 125,000 family members. Even assuming an interest cost on the use of the $230,000, the donor's net cost to change lives could be far less than $1 per person.

However, the donor understands that he risks not receiving any of his $230,000 back. His worst-case estimate is that he will create or strengthen 10,000 jobs for a total cost to him of $260,000, an average of $26 per job, or helping 10,000 families with 50,000 members to move out of poverty for about $5 a person. From a risked investment standpoint, the donor believes this is a great project.

Some microcredit providers can also increase financial leverage by accessing the savings of their borrowers. A large international microcredit provider stated in a confidential memorandum regarding its future capital that "approximately 75% of these amounts will come from client savings in our banks and from borrowing from the capital markets and 25% from donations." In other words, for every dollar, pound, or yen that a donor contributes, four times that amount will be available as loans. Although lower than the 12:1 leverage for the case in India discussed above, this is still excellent financial leverage.

Other types of financial leverage may also be possible, including letters of credit. Matching arrangements with other donors also can increase the power of a contribution another 25 to 200%. Grants to microcredit projects from governmental organizations are often contingent on an organization raising a certain percentage of the total project costs from private citizens. To gain maximum financial leverage, it is imperative to work with microcredit organizations that understand financial engineering and employ imaginative financial techniques.

Caution!

Lending to microcredit providers or using letters of credit on their behalf needs to be considered very carefully. It takes capital to grow a microcredit provider, and the more successful the provider, the more capital it needs to keep growing.

HIDDEN TRAPS

Microcredit is destined to fail when borrowers do not use their loans properly. A borrower who uses the loan to pay off another loan or buy non-income-producing items will not reap the benefits of credit. Nor will she be eligible for a second loan. If her husband steals and squanders her loan, she will not be able to build her business, and her domestic problems may escalate as well. In either case, she will be worse off after the loan than before. Since this is not in the best interests of either the borrowers or the lenders, many microcredit organizations educate borrowers about responsible use of credit, and they follow up with borrowers on a regular basis. Lenders who do not take these precautions may be setting a trap for both the borrowers and their microcredit programs.

However, if the microcredit provider looks like it will fail, decide to go out of business, or even reduce the amount of microloans it makes, then borrowers are likely to quit paying back their loans and the provider's noncollateralized microloan portfolio is likely to collapse. Therefore, it is unrealistic to expect that a loan you might make would be repaid by reducing the size of the organization's microloan portfolio. Instead, the microcredit organization would most likely try to pay back your loan by raising new funds from other donors or lenders. So, repayment from a microcredit provider is not as dependent on borrowers repaying their microloans as it is on the microcredit provider raising new money to repay your loan. Furthermore, similar to a business, as a microcredit provider goes further into debt, it increases the risk to its own financial well-being. If these risks are acceptable, you, like the lender in the above example, can exert tremendous financial leverage by lending money to a microcredit provider. Just be aware that it can be very risky, especially with a small organization.

One more lever remains, and it stems naturally from microcredit contributions with no additional work on your part. After you have employed all the financial levers you can, this lever further increases the impact of your investment.

The Sustained Change Lever

When a microbusiness succeeds or is strengthened, the entrepreneur and his or her family reap the benefits of immediate, usually sustained and often permanent, income increase. The children grow up healthier and better educated. The family's subsequent generations may be spared the poverty into which this generation was born. The entrepreneur who is making more money in turn spends more money for local goods and services, which upgrades the local economy and creates more jobs. This ripple effect becomes exponential through the generations. As children grow up more prosperous than the previous generation, they purchase more goods and services. Even more people become employed to meet the increased demand for nutritious food, education, transportation, decent housing, other basic needs, and some luxuries, such as indoor plumbing, holiday gifts, and modern appliances. As the proverb says, "A rising tide lifts all boats."

Realistic Expectations

For people who apply an investment mind-set to their giving, an important statistic to measure giving efficiency would be, "How many lives will I change on a long-term basis for the money I contribute?" Here is how Eric and I calculate an answer to that question when it comes to microcredit.

First, use the rule of thumb mentioned above: the total amount of borrowed funds required to improve a microbusiness and move a borrower up the economic ladder is roughly equal to the average annual income per capita of the borrower's country. According to the World Bank, in 2005 the average annual per capita incomes for the following countries were

Democratic Republic of Congo	$120
Republic of Rwanda	$230
India	$720
Republic of Honduras	$1,190
Ukraine	$1,520
Russian Federation	$4,460

Second, estimate how many times donations will circulate by being reloaned. If you are working with an excellent, self-sustaining organization, money eventually will circulate a minimum of 20 times (ten years of six-month loans). In other words, every $1,000 contributed eventually will provide at least $20,000 in microloans.

Third, each microbusiness supports a family, and it is reasonable to expect that families have an average of five members. So, multiplying the loan recycle rate (20) by the number of family members (5) means that every donation directly changes the lives of 100 children and adults. That 100 becomes part of the formula in the final step of the calculation. That last step is to divide the country's average annual per capita income by 100 to calculate the cost per person. This calculation yields an answer that is exactly 1% of a country's average annual per capita income.

COUNTRY	COST PER PERSON
Democratic Republic of Congo	$1.20
Republic of Rwanda	$2.30
India	$7.20
Republic of Honduras	$11.90
Ukraine	$15.20
Russian Federation	$44.60

Clearly, these numbers are approximations, but to help people bring themselves out of deadly poverty for a cost of $1.20 per person seems incredible. Even $44.60 a person sounds ridiculously low. These figures may seem too good to be true, but they are realistic. Recall the cost-per-life (CPL) calculation described in Chapter 2. CPL becomes amazingly low with microcredit because loans are paid back and the money is recycled to help yet another family of poor people. This is why supporting microcredit is so appealing to donors with business acumen. When you crunch the numbers, it is hard to imagine any other humanitarian service that can produce such impressive results.

Of course, the CPL described above represents the ideal outcome. One must also be aware of the fine print disclosing possible limitations. A donor's funds are most efficient if the entire donation goes directly into microloans, not overhead, and if the total donation is invested in a program that is sustainable or close to sustainability. Also, as a typical loan term is three to six months, your money needs to circulate up to 20 times to reach projected outcomes. It could take a decade before your return on investment reaches its full potential. Still, taking all these factors into consideration, we have found no other humanitarian work that delivers more in terms of changed lives for lower cost than microcredit.

The cost analysis to change a life is described in more detail in Appendix D, which shows how to adjust the numbers for various situations. I developed this calculation to help inform my personal giving. My rule of thumb is that it takes a net cost of about 1% of the average annual per capita income of a country to move one person up the economic ladder using microcredit.

As an example, I supported a program in Ghana, a country with an average annual per capita income of $450. Geneva Global, a donor service organization, arranged for a $50,000 grant to a local microcredit organization to make microloans averaging $95 for 500 borrowers who were HIV-positive, suffering from AIDS, or dealing with AIDS in their families. In addition, the grant provided basic business skills training for 300 women, most of them widows. Assuming five members per family, the initial cost to help suffering people improve their lives is $20 per person. Then, as the money is recycled into more loans, the cost per person drops dramatically to about $3 or $4 per person (assuming borrowers go through three or four loan cycles). In addition, families in the program would receive business training plus social services that would help them deal with AIDS-related emotional, social, and financial havoc.

By now I should not be so amazed at the phenomenal bottom line, but I continue to be. Every time I run the numbers on a microcredit project, the net cost to change lives is so low that my engineering mind tells me I must have miscalculated. But it is no mistake. The results are that good.

Seize the Moment

Why are the results from microcredit so astounding on a financial basis? I believe this happens for two of the reasons that it occasionally occurs with investment opportunities in for-profit business. First, investors realize their highest returns in the earliest stages of a new business concept. Many of the world's wealthiest people are those who invested in unknown ideas or unknown companies that are now familiar to all, such as computer software (Microsoft), retail stores (Wal-Mart), or Internet search engines (Google). The people with the idea, and the early investors and financiers, make the big money, but they also put in the most work and take on the most risk. Later investors realize lower returns, but take on much less risk.

However, there is another point in time when tremendous amounts of money can be made. Late in business cycles, industries have finished building infrastructure, and in fact may be overbuilt. At that point those industries can become capital-starved because the earlier investors are not content with low returns and move elsewhere. New investors come in and snap up companies and assets for a fraction of their previous value. If those industries rebound, the new investors stand to make huge returns, especially if they leverage their investments.

Microcredit is currently in that late-stage position. The people who had the idea and the early philanthropic investors and financiers invested millions of hours and dollars. They tested microcredit methods and techniques, developed the technology, and built the infrastructure of today's microcredit organizations. (See Appendix A.) They have uncovered a huge market demand and have proven that microcredit works. Now, late-stage microcredit supporters can reap outlandishly high returns for low risk by taking advantage of three decades of investments and hard work by others. Microcredit is capital-starved because few people know about it and understand how and why it works. By providing some of this capital, you can help poor people advance their small businesses with sweat equity and bootstrap loans. With loans, not handouts, they can achieve economic stability and the dignity that stems from solving their own problems.

Today's philanthropists can enable people to lift themselves out of poverty for less than the cost of a cup of coffee. Even if the cost were 10 cups or 100 cups, it would still be astounding. History illustrates that just throwing more money at the poverty problem is not the solution. Poverty's grip on the world's most vulnerable people will loosen only if money is invested wisely.

The financial levers available with microcredit are powerful, and you can move the world by using them. Other levers are the genius of microcredit methods, the dedication of field staff, and the tenacity of poor entrepreneurs. Although world poverty is powerful, the levers are even stronger.

" Lasting peace cannot be achieved unless large population groups find ways in which to break out of poverty. Microcredit is one such means. "

—OLE DANBOLT MJØS

NOBEL COMMITTEE DIRECTOR,
ANNOUNCING THAT DR. MUHAMMAD YUNUS
HAD WON THE NOBEL PEACE PRIZE

CHAPTER 6

MICROCREDIT PLUS

Eric Thurman

More than a century ago, Andrew Carnegie was the richest businessman in the world, controlling the most extensive and complete system of iron and steel industries ever managed by an individual. His landmark innovation was cheap and efficient mass production of steel rails for railroad lines. Yet he is remembered more for the libraries and schools he funded than the companies he founded. Effective giving can be the greatest achievement of a lifetime.

A case in point would be the important work of improving healthcare, as promoted by the Gates Foundation and others, which could be delivered as an additional benefit along with microloans. We call this pairing of lending with other services "Microcredit Plus," an excellent approach because poverty often involves more than lack of money. While some income-related problems such as hunger simply disappear as families move out of extreme poverty, other problems persist. This is where the "Plus" comes in.

GETTING THE NAME RIGHT

Nomenclature is a heated topic among some practitioners. Many argue passionately that the movement should
be called *microfinance* because poor people need savings
and insurance as well as loans. Others claim that *microcredit* should be the preferred term because lending is
the core of the movement. The authors favor *microcredit*
for that reason. Originally the industry was known as
microenterprise development, or *MED*. (See Glossary for
an expanded list of definitions.) In common use, all
three terms get used interchangeably despite their distinct meanings.

We have coined an alternative term because the
industry lacked an umbrella word to describe the wide
variety of extra benefits that are often linked with
microloans. These added services range from health to
literacy, and many other social programs. The language
we advocate is *Microcredit Plus*, to explain all types of situations in which poor people access additional services
in conjunction with their loans.

Lending programs are an ideal context for delivering
added services because the programs have established trust
with the borrowers, opening them to new ideas. Since credit
groups gather at regular intervals, it takes little, if any, additional expense to build extra services into those meetings.
Because of the impeccable ethics of good microcredit programs, participants are not concerned about the bribes and

thefts that are the scourge of many social service programs. Health and literacy programs, legal information, and even farming tips have all been delivered successfully alongside microcredit. Savings and insurance are among the most common add-ons to lending programs; they decrease the vulnerability of poor families to emergencies, disasters, and unexpected expenses.

Lagniappe

Lagniappe is Creole for "a little bit extra for the same price." Microcredit Plus is the *lagniappe* that allows such things as abusive cultural practices to be overcome. One example is the dreadful tradition found in some African societies whereby a widow must be ritually "cleansed" by forced sex with one or more of her deceased husband's brothers. It takes education and cultural change to break such customs, and this has been accomplished through Microcredit Plus programs. In villages where microcredit programs include HIV/AIDS education, this superstition has been modified into a symbolic ritual accepted as a substitute for physical assault. This modification greatly improves the quality of life of the members of the microcredit group and the personal dignity of the widows, and it can influence the social norms of entire communities. Improving life for a vulnerable woman may require more than just loaning her money for a small business. Microcredit Plus services enable her to earn and command respect in her personal life as well.

Strategic alliances with other organizations are another way microcredit groups add extra features to their lending. Habitat for Humanity partnered with Opportunity International to combat AIDS in sub-Saharan Africa. Through that cooperative arrangement, AIDS orphans worked on Habitat housing projects and learned valuable construction skills. Opportunity International clients also mentored and trained the young people so they were able to use microloans to start their own businesses. Microcredit providers have joined forces with various groups to provide childhood immunizations, malaria prevention, AIDS awareness, and a wide array of other services.

I was leading Opportunity International in the early 1990s when the Iron Curtain fell. Stacie Schrader, then the country director in Russia, and Ken Vander Weele, regional director for Eastern Europe, did a superlative job of setting up the first microcredit programs across the former Soviet Union. The result of their work remains the largest microfinance network in Russia as well as in several other countries in the region. I recall visiting one Opportunity office in Rostov-on-Don in the south of Russia. There, people who had relied on employment at state-owned factories from the old planned economy suddenly needed to find new lives as self-employed, entrepreneurial capitalists. They quickly adapted and did very well with their microloans and small businesses. In the first few months, however, Stacie noticed that many of the borrowers desperately needed legal advice to navigate confusing and constantly changing government regulations. Stacie arranged for a lawyer to be available one night each week to answer registration and tax questions. This service was provided free to the borrowers.

The Cult of the Expert

Stacie Schrader's astute response to these changing requirements grew out of her awareness of a unique local situation.
This approach is far superior to dreaming up interventions in
a developed country and then foisting them on a faraway community. This is the difference between the bottom-up and the
top-down approaches discussed in Chapter 2.

Governments and so-called experts often view poverty as a
problem stemming from national underdevelopment. This
leads them to devise macroeconomic, or top-down, solutions
for the country's formal economy. They try to attack poverty
on a large scale, using techniques that regularly fail because
they concentrate on economic systems rather than on people.
Many solutions to poverty work best on a small scale in the
informal economy, or bottom-up.

Picture a foreign development expert visiting a remote
African village. He observes children with bloated bellies and
orange hair, unmistakable signs of protein deficiency. He does
not have to be a physician to make that diagnosis. So the
expert arranges to ship in protein-rich food supplements.
Village elders graciously accept and distribute the supplements to the mothers as directed, but they do not expect them
to be widely used. The mothers are already giving their children ample amounts of food. The children do not feel hungry,
so why would they want to eat this strange-tasting supplement? They think the expert did not recognize what was obvious to everyone in the village: when a mother notices her
child's hair turning orange, she knows her husband is cheating
on her. So she takes the child to a witch doctor who dispenses
the standard treatment, an amulet for the child to wear.

Changing entrenched traditional beliefs is not simple. Information must come from a trusted source, not from a foreign expert who takes little or no time to understand local culture and customs. Microcredit organizations, by contrast, routinely tap into local knowledge in shaping their programs. Educating a small group of borrowers can change the attitudes and actions of an entire village. Again, the cost is small since the borrowers already meet every week. Best of all, the microcredit leaders have credibility in the community.

Hunger and Nutrition

Freedom from Hunger is an international development organization working in 16 countries. It started in 1946 under the name Meals for Millions and produced Multi-Purpose Food, which is still used today in emergency relief situations. In the 1970s, the organization shifted its emphasis to health and nutrition programs for mothers and children. Since 1988, Freedom from Hunger has moved to being an integrated microcredit/health and nutrition education program. By 2005, this Microcredit Plus program was serving nearly 400,000 families in some of the world's poorest countries. The organization's experience in microcredit enhances its health programs and vice versa.

The United Nations estimates that approximately 850 million people in the world suffer from chronic hunger. The countries in which they live lack the social safety nets common in wealthier countries, such as soup kitchens, homeless shelters, and government programs. If a family cannot grow enough food or earn enough to buy food, there is nowhere to

A convenience store by Third World standards is often a small room attached to the owner's house. This woman operates her shop in Kinshasa, the capital of the Democratic Republic of Congo.

Igor at his drugstore in Volgodonsk, Russia that he developed using his microloan. Story in Chapter 9.

Even the largest markets in most of the world are made up of small vendors, like the stall run by this woman in Phnom Penh, Cambodia. Success depends on having variety and enough of the products that her customers want.

In the Dominican Republic, Crucita used her microloans to buy this oven as well as a freezer, washing machine, and motorcycle as capital investments for her small enterprises. As crude as these tools seem compared to modern appliances, they are earning her a livable income. Story in Chapter 5.

Mama Ndugu gives microcredit expert Peter Greer the largest yam of her harvest to show appreciation for all the help her microloan has been to her. This story from Rwanda is in Chapter 3.

Eric Thurman presides over the grand opening of Geneva Global's expanded facilities.

These women are collecting and recording payments from their microcredit group. They look far more prosperous than they are. The women, who live on the outskirts north of Nairobi, Kenya, are dressed in their only fine clothing because they consider their lending group meeting an important social event as well as a business session.

These children are so poor that none of them has shoes, but their brown uniforms mean that they are in school. They are singing and dancing to celebrate their hope for the future. Two years earlier, before an income program came to their village, none of them was receiving formal education.

Just a few tools and a small supply of material is all it takes for many people, like this cobbler in Bulgaria, to set up a business. Without a microloan, however, even those modest requirements are hopelessly out of reach for millions of people.

Many microentrepreneurs literally carry their business on their heads.

A microloan that supports a tiny business like this vegetable stand in Kenya benefits more than the borrower. It means the community has an ample supply of healthy, fresh food and farmers have a customer for their produce.

Lucy Billingsley, a successful businesswoman from Dallas, Texas recruited friends to help her set up a microlending program in Chiapas, Mexico. Here she is seen embracing a borrower. Story in Chapters 1 and 7.

Signing the papers for the first microloan issued at the opening of a new lending office in Volgodonsk, Russia. Story in Chapter 9.

The ability to weave artful mats is not only a creative talent, but also an excellent way to earn a living in India, where this woman used her microloan to buy the straw which she then dyed and wove.

Phil Smith discusses business with this borrower who runs a clothing kiosk in Nikopol, Ukraine. Story in Chapter 9.

Street vending is one of the most common forms of self-employment in poor communities. In Karachi, Pakistan, Eric Thurman talks with a worker known locally as a "cart man." He spends long hours every day pushing his rolling food stand through the streets of slums, but his income remains extremely low because he has such limited variety and small volume to sell. He needs counseling and a microloan to build his business.

Eric Thurman celebrates with a community of Pygmies in Burundi. Known locally as Batwa people, they were nomadic for generations and the poorest tribe in a country that is one of the five poorest nations on Earth. An income program raising animals makes it possible for them to establish permanent homes. Their quality of life is improving quickly.

These Russian babushkas (grandmothers) bake bread at home and then sell it from sidewalk stands. With microloans they are able to make as much as they can sell.

Professor Muhammad Yunus, winner of the Nobel Peace Prize. Upon accepting the prize, he said, "We are creating an entirely new generation that will be equipped to take their families way out of the reach of poverty. We want to make a break with the historical continuation of poverty."

In less developed countries the equivalent of a shopping mall is often an open air market. This "shoe store" is in Uganda.

Phil Smith as CEO of Tide West Oil Company, 1995. Story in Chapter 1.

People may be poor and may not have formal education, but they are, nonetheless, talented and highly entrepreneurial. Microcredit invests in people, like this woman in Burundi, so they can advance themselves and the generations that will follow them.

turn. Here again, Microcredit Plus programs are helping. By adding nutrition training to microcredit, borrowers learn how to solve their families' particular nutrition-related problems, ensuring that family members consume necessary amounts of the right types of food.

Business Training

When Phil and I met, I was CEO of Geneva Global. He was using Geneva to find and investigate microcredit projects he could support. We both learned a significant lesson from a grant he made of $22,000 to the faith-based Center for Community Transformation in the Philippines. As usual, we did extensive due diligence on the program, producing a forecast of expected outcomes. This proved to be one of the few times Geneva's estimates were far off the mark.

The grant was supposed to provide loans for 300 families and business training for 120 women. One year later, actual results were surprising. Loans went to 1,450 families, far exceeding expectations. The training component, however, seriously underachieved. Only 53 women received instruction in management, simple accounting, meat processing, and how to participate in a cooperative because there were not enough available trainers. That result taught us to check, at the outset, whether human resources are available to deliver programs we are about to fund. Analysis of actual results at the conclusion of a grant is an excellent teacher. It's important to know what happened.

This case study points out another type of Microcredit Plus: training to go with loans. Training can mean helping borrowers become better mechanics or seamstresses. It can be information transfer of more universal competencies such as bookkeeping and inventory control. Whether in a specific trade or general business expertise, training can greatly enhance a borrower's chance for success. Many microcredit providers insist that training is the most crucial additional service they can provide clients.

MICROCREDIT   IN ACTION

Fatoumata Monomata lives in Burkina Faso, one of the poorest countries in Africa where average life expectancy is only 44 years. Since childhood, she has known about a terrible disease called malaria, but she and her neighbors did not know how it was spread, how to protect themselves, when it would strike, and what kind of medicine would help. Malaria, a ruthless killer, swept through her village repeatedly, stealing the lives of countless children. Fatoumata feared for her children, but she had no idea how to protect them. She obtained a microloan along with information about nutrition and malaria from Freedom from Hunger. She used the loan to buy nuts and potatoes to sell. She increased her income enough to buy medicine, insecticide-treated mosquito nets, and nutritious food for her children. With her loans, she was able to get a wagon, which further increased her profits. Fatoumata shares her wagon and new knowledge with her neighbors so they too can improve their incomes and health.

Medical Care and Disease Prevention

Medical care is difficult for charities to deliver in places like Burkina Faso in West Africa. The population is scattered, and transportation and communication are mediocre, at best. When I was there some years ago, the entire country had only a few miles of paved roads. Understandably, people are suspicious of outsiders and anything they consider strange new ideas. Teaming medical services with microcredit, however, has proven an efficient, effective way to provide health and disease prevention information that borrowers and their communities can comprehend and use.

Preserving the Environment

Rural Hondurans in the region of Olanchito are still recovering from the devastation of Hurricane Mitch in 1998. Many water supplies remain polluted. Roads to the capital of Tegucigalpa often wash away during the rainy season. Farmers in this community continue to use outdated practices, which produce meager crop yields and damage the environment. Thick, biodiverse forests once covered the hills, but now the trees have been cut, logged, and burned. Peasants' agricultural practices destroy arable land and disrupt the ecological balance. According to one poor farmer, "I can only expect destruction for my family, because I am provoking it with my own hands. I put in my request, but the banks don't want to give me credit because I cannot guarantee the loan. I know what I am doing—as a person I know. I am destroying the land." This is a painful situation for both the people and the environment. Imagine trying to grow anything on inclines as steep as 70% without proper equipment and techniques.

In 2004, while I was CEO of Geneva Global Inc., I invited Phil to partner with a local nonprofit organization to provide a combination of services to several communities in Olanchito. It needed only $12,600 to increase lending through six community banks and hire two technical advisers. Geneva's due diligence on the grant looked at the experience of comparable projects and forecast that the impact would be nearly 1,000 people experiencing a 50% reduction in diarrhea and malnutrition, 600 people increasing their incomes by 25%, many women becoming incorporated into economic activities, and more than 100 farmers switching to farming methods that would not harm the environment. This is microcredit with big pluses for both health and ecology.

The situation just described in Honduras is repeated around the world. The pressing need to feed their hungry families drives millions of farmers to destroy ecosystems, deplete natural resources, wipe out entire species, and ultimately disrupt weather patterns. Microcredit in rural areas, combined with training in modern farming techniques, assistance in digging wells and constructing low-tech irrigation systems, and legal help in clearing property deeds can significantly decrease ecological damage and at the same time increase farmers' incomes and improve the health of their families.

Plus for Women

Microcredit empowers millions of women to support themselves and their children with dignity. In many countries women have no legal right to own property; they are merely chattel belonging to their husbands, brothers, and fathers. Those who have legal rights often do not know about them. If they do know, they are too poor to take their cases to court. Their plight is unimaginable if you have not visited such communities. In parts of Africa, a husband's death is a grief compounded by destitution. The dead man's brothers own his house, his land, perhaps even his wife. Many widows and their children have nothing, which leads to survival choices that are both dangerous and degrading. For thousands, the only survival option is prostitution. This is a heartrending reality I heard about often when I was leading Opportunity International and setting up Zambuko Trust, a microcredit agency in Zimbabwe. As one woman working on the streets of Harare put it, "Yes, I know about AIDS, but my children are hungry today. I won't die of AIDS for another few years."

That comment still haunts me. Desperate people like that young mother in Harare need good alternatives. Another woman living in the same city illustrates the contrast between the former situation and what happens when people have a better option. I met Terezia Mbaseri when visiting Zambuko Trust. Terezia is one of the most dynamic entrepreneurs I have been privileged to know. She and her husband lived in a mud hut, but she managed to put her five children through school by making and selling traditional straw brooms for the equivalent of 25 cents each. When her profits were not sufficient to pay all the school fees, she began selling soda from her front yard to passersby. That local version of a convenience store is known as a *tuck shop* because it is usually no more than a little stack of merchandise kept tucked in a corner of the seller's house. Next, Terezia bought a hen and began to sell its eggs as well. She was measuring progress one crate of soda and one new hen at a time. When Zambuko Trust opened, she was one of the first to apply for a loan. After a series of loans, she had developed two small grocery stores, a beauty salon, and a firewood business, and she told me she intended to keep opening new stores until she had a shopping mall! She moved from her mud hut to a modern house with indoor plumbing, electricity, and other amenities.

By the time I met Terezia, she employed 11 people who came from the countryside to earn money to send back to their destitute families. To help them, she built a dormitory in her yard where her employees could live rent free. Beyond that, she provided shelter in the same residence for a few infirm people. She regularly helped neighbors who could not help themselves, though she insisted that all able-bodied people work. Although she had already achieved a very comfortable living by local standards, she told me she wanted to keep expanding her businesses so that more people could have jobs. This grandmother of 15 said she had no plans to retire.

Church Growth

Members of a church in Tulsa, Oklahoma, teamed with HOPE International to establish a new microcredit organization in southern Russia. After the church had already trained 40 Russian ministers and established several new congregations in the area, it realized that the initiative would eventually stall unless it found a way for those congregations to grow and pay their ministers without relying on perpetual funding from the outside. The church members raised $500,000 to start a microcredit program providing loans to the ministers, church members, and others in the communities the churches serve. Over time, those loans will help the Russian churches become financially independent as their members improve their incomes.

Churches all over the world are rethinking their approach to missions. I have seen a growing movement of churches becoming involved in AIDS by providing hospice care for people who are sick and orphan care for the children left behind when their parents die from the disease. In a similar way, churches around the world are increasing their programs to end poverty, one family at a time. Best-selling author Rick Warren, who wrote *The Purpose Driven Life,* is advocating this with a campaign he calls "The PEACE Plan." PEACE is an acronym with the "A" standing for "Assist the Poor." He is encouraging churches to use microcredit and other programs to break the painful cycle of families trapped in poverty for generation after generation. Microcredit delivered in partnership with churches provides both spiritual care and community development.

Microcredit Plus

Entrepreneurs are among the most inventive people in the world. It is amazing to travel the world and see all the imaginative ways they create items of value and sell them to earn a living for their families. It is no surprise then that the people who gravitate to work with these entrepreneurs through microcredit programs are also opportunistic in the best sense of that word. They notice what is happening in a community. When more than credit is needed to help entrepreneurs build a good life, they add "Plus" services. There is no convenient list of eight or ten types of Plus services that cover every situation. People who administer microcredit are inventive as they custom-design add-ons to ensure that borrowers get ahead in life.

BORROWER "PLUS"

Sometimes benefits added to microcredit are not designed by the lending organization, but occur spontaneously when borrowers spread their good fortune out into the community. Oleg Bulgaru, of Chisinau, Moldova, took that initiative. Imprisoned under Communism, he had no way to earn a living once he was set free. With a microloan from HOPE International, he began a furniture assembly business which provided his family with secure housing, adequate food, and a small savings account for the children's education.

A second loan led to growing profits, enabling Oleg and his four business partners, all former prisoners like himself, to provide newly released prisoners with clothes, shoes, and even to help with their rent until they find jobs. People still behind bars receive food, medicines, books, and clothing. The business now fully supports the work Oleg calls his ministry, which he is eager to take to still more prisons.

Recently HOPE International honored Oleg as the borrower who accomplished the most with his or her loan in 2006.

You have to applaud that kind of ingenuity. It never would have occurred to me, for instance, that an adaptation of microcredit could change the lives of those suffering from Hansen's disease, commonly known as leprosy. Yet, at Geneva Global we found and arranged funding for such a program in the Philippines. While the number of people suffering from Hansen's is thankfully declining, society still stigmatizes its remaining victims. In the Philippines, it was discovered that when people with Hansen's have an income, they are treated differently; they are accepted and can be integrated back into their communities. So a program was developed for exactly that purpose. Every day, somewhere in the world, a new benefit is linked with microcredit.

When I first met Phil, I learned that one of his passions is to make money "work hard." He insists on this, whether it is money he is investing or giving. He wants his money to deliver results. No wonder he favors Microcredit Plus programs. He has given to microcredit programs that help all kinds of people, from farmers to mothers of handicapped children. Another of his priorities is encouraging formation and expansion of healthy churches that stabilize communities and embrace people. Other donors I have known have passions to confront different poverty-related issues, such as AIDS orphans, human trafficking, sexploitation, or disadvantaged women. You may want to reflect on what types of human suffering matter most to you. Chances are good that someone, somewhere, has adapted a microcredit program to address that problem. As you think about microcredit, remember that microcredit programs can have many pluses, particularly in the world's poorest places.

"*In fact, acts of charity can be dangerous because givers can feel good about actions that actually accomplish very little, or even create dependency. The result is that their sense of satisfaction takes away any motivation to seek more creative long-range development strategies. Overcoming an attitude of charity is a difficult task because it requires givers to demand more of themselves than good will.*"

—JOHN M. PERKINS, *BEYOND CHARITY*

CHAPTER 7

BEYOND GOOD INTENTIONS

Phil Smith

A t this point, it might seem to you that microcredit is fool-proof. Lest it appear that you cannot go wrong by supporting microcredit, it is important to fully describe the reality. Thinking back to my initial involvement in microcredit, the trip down that road was sometimes rather bumpy.

I vividly remember the frustration of eight of my acquaintances during their first attempts to participate in microcredit. They gave several microloans directly to impoverished Russians to help them start small businesses, such as beekeeping and a delivery service. Unfortunately, the factors of distance, language, and unforeseen business problems began taking their toll. The clients seemed sincere in their desire to repay their loans, but their installments arrived irregularly if at all. The expression "The devil is in the details" came alive as my friends' good intentions turned into apprehensions.

The purpose of this chapter is to walk you through reliable ways you can connect with microcredit while avoiding the pitfalls. Microcredit is not as simple as sending money and a half-page loan agreement to an entrepreneurial poor person in a faraway country. That may not be legal, and it certainly is not wise.

Let Your Preferences Guide Your Choices

Before examining your options, pause and reflect for a moment. You may want to take out a piece of paper and write a few notes. Although I can describe excellent ways to take part in the microcredit movement, only you can define your personal interests. Jot down as much as you can about what you would like to accomplish through microcredit. For those of you with families, this could provide an excellent opportunity to discuss issues that can either divide or join a family in its giving ventures. Here are a few questions to stimulate your thinking:

- What do you want to contribute: your money, personal skills and influence, or time? It might very well be a combination of these.
- Do you want to make a one-time donation to "put your toe in the water," or are you considering a long-term commitment?
- What is the cumulative amount of donations you might be willing to give to microcredit over the next few years?

- Are you interested in solving a range of poverty-related problems, or would you prefer to concentrate exclusively on helping people increase their incomes?
- Are you interested in a particular region or country?
- Is there a particular type of person you are motivated to help, such as women abandoned by their husbands and left to care for their children with no source of income, families devastated by HIV/AIDS, farmers, or some other special group?

Knowing your preferences on issues like these will serve as a guide as you learn more about the options presented later in this chapter.

Your giving options cluster under three broad categories. No matter what cause you wish to support, microcredit or anything else, there are only three ways you can channel your resources. Professional fundraisers know this triplet well. They describe each part with the letter T: time, treasure, and talent. These are the only items anyone can contribute. A more elegant way of describing these options is that we can give:

- Our financial resources—money and credit
- Our personal resources—skills, relationships, and influence
- Our lives—donating hours and possibly even years of our time

In many cases, obviously, giving involves a combination of all three. The first way most people participate in microcredit is by giving money.

SISTERS ESTABLISH
A SPECIAL FUND

Two sisters from Chicago visited a small microcredit organization in Nagpur, India. After spending several days with the staff and meeting the borrowers, they decided to support the organization. After raising funds from their church and family, they specified that the money be lent to impoverished mothers who did not meet the organization's regular lending requirements. The staff was delighted to have a special fund for women who were too risky to be included in the regular loan pool. The risk was not their extreme poverty; it was their social isolation. They had no friends who would vouch for them.

The sisters were pleased that 75% of these borrowers successfully repaid their loans and increased their families' incomes. For regular microcredit programs 75% would be an unacceptable repayment rate, but this was a special niche program for people whose only other hope was begging. Even with the 25% loan losses, the sisters had made an excellent philanthropic investment. The international organization they had formerly supported took at least 30% of donations for overhead. By giving directly to the local implementer, their contribution was 5% more efficient. In addition, they reached deeper into poverty to provide a way out for mothers in extreme circumstances.

Donor Option One:
Give to Grassroots Organizations

An ideal way to participate in microcredit is to connect with small, effective organizations in developing countries. Your donations often will have the greatest impact, and you are likely to develop personal friendships with the organizations' leaders. However, finding and evaluating the best local providers entails a great deal of research and likely one or more trips to a developing country. Geographic, cultural, and language barriers will also complicate communications with the organization's leaders. Accounting systems and financial report formats differ widely among countries, making them hard to comprehend. Even numbering systems go by different names in some countries. For the uninitiated, keeping up with financial discussions in other parts of the world is bewildering.

Furthermore, U.S. citizens face strict limitations on transferring money overseas for charitable purposes because of restrictions by the federal government that are meant to limit terrorism, drug trafficking, and money laundering. For instance, the Office of Foreign Assets Control has legal requirements that restrict money transfers in order to enforce U.S. sanctions. You also will find banks unwilling to transfer money to countries that are on government restriction lists. Citizens of other countries have their own government regulations and restrictions to consider. If you are willing to do the work required to legally surmount these barriers, you are positioned to have a wonderful experience of witnessing how your contribution is changing lives in a specific place. If you are not qualified or prepared to be so pioneering with your giving, you have many other options.

Donor Option Two:
The MicroCredit Solutions Fund

In recent years I supported a number of microcredit projects that were discovered and researched by Geneva Global Inc. Geneva brings business-grade due diligence to the analysis of projects in developing countries. I have supported many Microcredit Plus projects, providing loans while simultaneously correcting one or more of the ills aggravated by poverty. I like taking advantage of the millions of dollars invested by those who created Geneva for evaluating their own philanthropic choices, as well as assisting donors who desire careful due diligence. Geneva has developed an uncommon ability to investigate grassroots programs in any corner of the globe. I could see, however, how it might go one step further. When Eric was CEO of Geneva Global, I asked the organization to design a special fund just for microcredit, so that anyone who was interested could have easy access to the best local projects run by groups who had no representatives in wealthy countries. I asked that the fund

- Work directly with the best *local microcredit providers* in developing countries
- Emphasize reaching people in the *lower levels of poverty*, which means programs often will include extra services such as disease prevention and community development
- Accept *contributions of any amount*, with project-designation privileges for those who make substantial contributions
- Direct most of the fund to microloans and related services effectively *bypassing unproductive overhead costs*

It was a tall order. In addition, I audaciously suggested one more element—a matching component to make the fund even more attractive to potential donors. In other words, for every dollar given by donors, more than a dollar would be delivered directly to projects through matching funds.

Eric challenged his colleagues to design a fund that would remove barriers to giving for microcredit projects by meeting all the standards I outlined. In the fall of 2005, Geneva launched the MicroCredit Solutions Fund, which was underwritten with a 25% match to increase each donation. The fund accepts donations of any size, and people giving $25,000 or more may designate their donation for a specific project within the fund. Donors receive reports showing the results of their giving expressed in both financial and life-change indicators.

The fund's first project was with URWEGO, a microcredit organization in Rwanda that became self-sustaining in 2005 and whose goal was to serve more poor entrepreneurs. In the local dialect, URWEGO means ladder. The stated aim of the organization is to help people climb the ladder of economic empowerment. Because of the unique difficulties in Rwanda, URWEGO's parent organization invested several million dollars in the process of setting up the lending program and establishing the initial loan portfolio. A donor to the MicroCredit Solutions Fund designated $500,000 to the project. This amount was given through a U.S. microcredit organization with special expertise in Rwanda, which purchased a minority ownership of URWEGO by injecting all of the $500,000 as new capital for microloans. That investment produced a side benefit: the added capital qualified URWEGO for further financing from other sources, which helped the organization grow even faster. This transaction provided enough capital to serve approximately 16,000 new borrowers a year, well into the future.

Donor Option Three:
Give to an International Organization

This is a popular option for both large and small donations. In 2006, John and Jacque Weberg announced their commitment to a legacy gift of $5 million annually for a decade to Opportunity International. In 2005, Pierre Omidyar, eBay founder, his wife, Pam, and two retired mutual-fund managers pledged a total of $9 million to the Grameen Foundation USA. The Omidyars' $4 million gift was made through their investment vehicle, the Omidyar Network. The other $5 million was pledged by Janet McKinley, retired chair of the Income Fund of America, and her husband George Miller. Like the Webergs, the Omidyars are increasing their support for microcredit. They recently gave $100 million to Tufts University earmarked for use in microcredit programs internationally.

Miller, McKinley, the Omidyars, and the Webergs chose the method that most donors, large and small alike, use to make microloans. They made qualifying tax-deductible (according to U.S. tax code) contributions to an international microcredit nonprofit organization. The largest of these organizations have fundraising offices in Europe and Asia as well as in North America. Many of them are listed in Appendix B.

Knowing as much as possible about the goals and financial histories of the organizations will help you select the one best suited to your giving objectives. You will find that some international microcredit providers set up their own local organizations and community banks, whereas others partner with local microcredit providers. Partnerships may include the exchange of technical expertise, loan capital, or both. Donors should investigate the organization's mission. Does it provide only microcredit to as many people as possible, or does it provide Microcredit Plus services as well? Does it focus on the poorest of the poor, or does it work with the more easily accessible working poor? Overhead is another important consideration.

As with other nonprofit organizations, microcredit donors may be supporting an expensive home office in a developed country, regional offices on different continents, and the local offices that deliver the program. This, combined with fundraising expenses, can bring overhead costs to 50% of your donation. Therefore, you need to understand how much of your donation goes to microloans and how much to sustaining the organization. To determine the impact of your giving on the people you want to help, you may wish to calculate the cost per life changed detailed in Chapter 2.

Larger organizations have found that some donors who are reluctant to give money are willing to loan it for no interest or for very low interest rates. Some of these organizations offer bonds, loan guarantees, or other financial instruments. These may be excellent methods for some people to become involved with microcredit. As always, do enough due diligence to ensure that you are making a prudent loan you will not be forced to reclassify later as a donation. Also, take care to understand the tax effects of loans versus donations.

Donor Option Four:
Give Your Skills as Well as Your Money

Lucy Billingsley, the Dallas real estate developer mentioned in Chapter 1, became excited when she learned about microcredit. She recruited other Dallas women to host breakfasts and coffees to raise money for microloans for women in the Mexican state of Chiapas. They connected with Alternative Solidaria, a local organization they met through its partner, the Grameen Foundation. This allowed the Dallas women to provide loans directly through the local Mexican microcredit organization. After raising several hundred thousand dollars, Lucy and a group of other women visited Chiapas to see what they were supporting. They immediately recognized the need: many of the village women had never worn shoes or had indoor plumbing. Some of the women spent half of every day combing the mountainside for fallen branches, because they could not afford to buy firewood. These women had good ideas for generating income, but they did not have the cash to start microbusinesses. In contrast, villagers who had received microloans in the past had visibly improved their incomes and lives. The Dallas women returned home with even more enthusiasm, and they immediately devised plans to expand the project.

As Lucy proved, her leadership skills were as valuable as her financial contributions. Lucy's decision to form a committee to provide microloans to people in another country is a powerful model for solving poverty across the border and spreading the joy of accomplishment within a social network. Her ability to form partnerships allowed her group to find the best local microcredit provider.

MICROCREDIT IN ACTION

In 1985, David Valle, then a catcher for the Seattle Mariners, decided to play winter baseball in the Dominican Republic. After his first game there, David and his wife Vicky walked out of the ballpark and were immediately surrounded by a crowd of young children. Ballplayers are often met by kids gathering autographs, but David quickly realized these boys and girls did not want his signature. They were hungry and begging for food. That night David and Vicky made a commitment to return to the Dominican Republic to do whatever they could to make a difference. Esperanza International is their fulfillment of that commitment.

Esperanza, which means hope in Spanish, focuses on well-proven solutions that enable families to help themselves. Along with other social service providers, Esperanza gives poor families access to microcredit, health care, education, business training, and vocational training. Not forgetting its roots, Esperanza uses baseball to keep in touch with various communities. It built a baseball stadium in the Dominican Republic that would be the envy of most U.S. minor league teams.

Draw upon your skills as Lucy did—each of us has distinct talents and experience to offer. Your personal network may be as valuable as your knowledge. You can connect people who have the capacity to give with microcredit groups that are ready to grow. One successful businessman who regularly syndicates investments and has trusted relationships at money center banks is doing this. By making an introduction, he unlocked hundreds of millions of dollars in inexpensive borrowing for a large international microcredit organization. As financial engineering and borrowed funds play a larger role in expanding loan portfolios, savvy business people have a great deal to contribute.

MICROCREDIT IN ACTION

Jim Bergman is an achiever. For most of his adult life he has been a successful venture capitalist. Now he is semiretired. Exactly what that means is unclear, because he is as active as ever. In some cases, the only difference is that he now makes his conference calls from home instead of an office.

When Jim and his wife Judy decided to invest themselves in microcredit, they did just that. They invested themselves. They took repeated trips overseas to visit organizations they were supporting. From his decades of experience growing companies, Jim realized that many of his corporate development skills could further enhance what were already great microcredit organizations. Four African microcredit providers, in Ghana, Kenya, Malawi, and Zambia, have added him to their boards, and he is helping each of them convert to banks. He tries to schedule board meetings on adjacent dates and says he manages to attend most sessions. Accustomed to holding seats on boards of companies where he had investments, Jim is now doing something similar by coaching African microcredit organizations.

Donor Option Five:
Give Your Time Along with Everything Else

Remember, you have only three ways to give: treasure, time, and talent. Fortunately, whatever your preference, you can find ways to affiliate with the microcredit organizations that can help you meet your goals.

If you are someone who can add value, I urge you to search until you find a place where you can connect with your skills and energy in addition to your donations.

Donor Option Six:
Start a Microcredit Program

Marshall Saunders began his career by leasing service stations for Shell Oil Company and then entered the real estate business by leasing shopping centers. After years of corporate success, he became a director for two microcredit organizations. Fascinated with the concept of microcredit, Marshall founded Grameen de la Frontera, in the state of Sonora, Mexico, that was serving nearly 4,000 borrowers by April 2005. The program achieved operational sustainability in 2005 and opened a second branch in the same state in 2006.

People like Saunders have founded many microcredit organizations. The learning curve can be steep, and unexpected challenges such as civil war and hyperinflation can add exotic complications rarely faced in ordinary business. It can be thrilling to overcome such obstacles. Administration costs can soar out of control, and the simplest-sounding business practice can prove to be culturally unacceptable. Carefully crafted business plans become unrealistic overnight. If your pioneering spirit leads you along this path, resources in Appendix C will help you avoid some of the pitfalls and increase the likelihood of success.

You are getting close to the prize. You have identified your giving priorities. You have decided what you want to give: time, talent, treasure, or a combination of the three. You think you are now ready to make your final choice, but first stop to consider a few essential items before you make your grand leap.

Due Diligence

First-rate investors always ask many due diligence questions before plunking down their cash. The same types of questions should be asked when considering which microcredit organizations to support. By making the appropriate queries, you can find programs that meet both your philanthropic motives and performance expectations. Knowing the right questions whittles a long list of possibilities down to a manageable few. Here are several starter questions:

- *What is the mission? Who does it help?* What are the expected outcomes?
- *Does the staff understand the local culture and marketplace?* No one knows better than people who grew up in the community.
- *How are borrowers selected? How deeply is the program reaching into poverty?* Be alert for "mission drift." Sometimes

groups that claim they are helping the poor actually are serving the middle class because larger loans are easier to manage.

- *How are borrowers qualified?* Few small businesses succeed without a motivated entrepreneur. Yet even the most motivated may fail if the market is saturated or no market exists for goods or services they sell.
- *What is the measure of success?* This measure should be positive change in the borrowers' lives, not in the lending institution's statistics. While it is important to track how many people pay back their loans, it is even more important to track whether borrowers are working their way out of poverty.
- *What percentage of your donations will be used for overhead?* It takes infrastructure to deliver a microcredit program, of course, but you deserve to know how your money will be used so you can decide if you approve.
- *Does the organization have a history of forming sustainable local programs without remaining dependent on anyone from outside the community?* The technical term is *sustainability*, but the principle is durability. You need to understand if the program will last long term without support from outside.

Question until You Learn the Unexpected

I wanted to support a local microcredit provider with three community banks in Honduras. The director said $6,000 would accomplish all of the program objectives. I offered

$3,000 more, intending to add a little cushion and further ensure success. To my surprise, the director refused, saying the banks did not have the staff to qualify additional borrowers and monitor their loans. I needed to hear that. Instead of improving the program, trying to handle too much money would have made it weaker.

Virtually every project I have investigated has had hidden surprises—some good, some bad. Just like with financial investments, the better due diligence you perform, the better results you can expect.

DEMAND
OUTSTRIPS SUPPLY

In 2004, a microcredit program opened in the Democratic Republic of Congo. After ten months, it had 2,400 borrowers whose loans averaged $76. In a 2005 report, a field officer wrote, "We can't possibly keep up with demand with the limited funding that we currently have. In fact, we'll have to stop at 800 borrowers in Kisangani unless additional funding is secured. Already, we're having to turn people away, and our loan officers reported just yesterday that this could even be a security risk. People desperate to receive this assistance have threatened the staff, 'Why won't you help us too?' It is remarkable that so many desperately want and can take advantage of this hand up and escape from the demoralizing hand-outs."

An Unmet Need Equals
an Untapped Opportunity

Have you ever noticed how the worlds of business and charity are sometimes in opposite corners? When people lack an important service, nonprofit groups say it is a big problem to be solved. Yet, the view is reversed in business. If you find a group of people who need an important service, mobile telephones for instance, that is a wonderful discovery and a market opportunity. Looking at microcredit with a business mind-set reveals a marvelous opportunity. Demand far outstrips supply.

Reading this book will not make you an expert on microcredit, but by now you have your arms around the main issues. You see the potential. You understand why local lending can do what national economic development programs cannot. Considering the colossal damage poverty does to families and societies, the next chapter contains some painful material. The good news is that poverty can be defeated, and you can join the battle knowing that good actions can prevail where good intentions fail.

" Massive poverty and obscene inequality are such terrible scourges of our times . . . that they have to rank alongside slavery and apartheid as social evils. "

—NELSON MANDELA,
FORMER PRESIDENT OF SOUTH AFRICA

CHAPTER 8

A THOUSAND BATTLES, A THOUSAND VICTORIES

Eric Thurman

In the 1990s, the international business community made a bestseller out of an ancient book, *The Art of War*, written by Sun Tzu, a Chinese general from the sixth century BC. It is the oldest military treatise in print. His tough-minded strategies predate Machiavelli by nearly two millennia. Leaders, both noble and nefarious, have turned to Sun Tzu's principles when dealing with conflict or competition. What would Sun Tzu say to those of us determined to triumph over the beast of poverty? He might reply with one of his most quoted statements: "Know thyself, know thy enemy. A thousand battles, a thousand victories." Another time he puts it this way: "If you know the enemy and know yourself you need not fear the results of a hundred battles."

The world is engaged in mortal combat with poverty. Poverty is not exclusively a financial problem. It is the leading cause of premature death in the world, affecting health, nutrition, and safety. Sun Tzu would say that to defeat poverty, we must thoroughly understand it. We need to know what feeds poverty, how it thrives on ignorance and apathy; and we must be warned about poverty's ability to wait us out until we become discouraged and give up. Perhaps that is why it is always a profound moment when anyone encounters devastating poverty up close for the first time. Phil Smith tells this story of his awakening during a trip with his daughter to the Dominican Republic:

"Like many tourists, we landed at the airport and took a shuttle directly to the beautiful Casa de Campo resort. We enjoyed tennis, golf, snorkeling, and trapshooting. Unlike other tourists, however, we wanted to visit sugarcane fields. I was curious about them since sugar is an important part of the country's economy. On a previous trip to Australia I had enjoyed watching state-of-the-art machines cut cane over thousands of square miles. I wanted to compare harvesting techniques.

"My first clue that this would be a very different experience came when we had difficulty finding anyone willing to take us to the cane fields. Finally, with a big tip, I persuaded a reluctant driver. As we came around the last dusty turn, we were stunned. Instead of huge modern machines, we saw hundreds of near-naked Haitians swinging machetes under the blistering sun. After chopping, they hauled the stalks to mule-drawn wagons. It was hard labor under harsh conditions, and the sawlike blades of the giant grass left the workers covered with cuts. Our driver told us that the men worked all day in subhuman conditions. Those who become ill or are heard complaining are sent back across the border to Haiti. Plenty of other Haitians are willing to take their place. The mules, explained the driver, are of more value than the men because they are harder to replace."

No matter how widely traveled wealthy people are, they are almost always shielded from the everyday lives of the poor and poverty's harsh realities. I invite you to tour the urban slums or indigent countrysides anywhere in the developing world to see, firsthand, what a struggle daily life is for hundreds of millions of people. Friends often ask me whether it is depressing to visit impoverished communities, but, to the contrary, I look forward to every trip. One reason is that I know I am there to bring improvement. The other reason is how appealing the people are. In every depressed community, I find people who are delightful and generous, lovable and resourceful. I often find that poor people are more open than those of us who have more resources, and it is a special pleasure to be among them.

In our mission to defeat poverty, we must case the enemy stronghold. At times it will be tempting to turn away from excruciatingly painful sights, but our strategies must include exploring, even spying on, the adversary. Throughout this book we have stressed positive stories of how poor people find new lives through microcredit. In the next few pages, by contrast, we will expose poverty at its ugliest to understand and, ultimately, break its power.

The Magnitude of Poverty

We can easily get lost in a maze of statistics about poverty, so I will highlight only a few key figures. First, it's important to know how data are tabulated, which greatly affects how they are interpreted. I am often asked, "Why do you worry so much about poor people in foreign countries; don't we have poor people here?" The answer is both yes and no, depending on whether the data are tabulated in *relative* or *absolute* terms. *Absolute* poverty compares people according to a fixed standard: how many calories they consume each day, or how many dollars a day they have for living expenses. *Relative* poverty, by contrast, compares different economic classes within a single country.

This distinction between *absolute* and *relative* poverty explains why I concentrate my efforts in less developed countries; in *absolute* terms, that is where all the poorest people are. If you take low-income Americans who are below the U.S. poverty line—a *relative* measurement—they are still among the richest people in the world in *absolute* terms.

Have you heard the colloquial expression, "I wonder how the 'other half' lives?" The "other half" refers to the gap between the haves and the have-nots, the privileged and the underclass. Worldwide, the "haves," who hold more than half of the world's wealth, make up just 10% of the global population. To be exact, the wealthiest 10% of people on Earth possess 54% of the income. The remaining 90% of people divide up the remaining 46%. Further analysis of poverty statistics shows that 40% of the world's entire population lives on less than $2 per day. There are about 2.5 billion people in that group who struggle to survive on just 5% of the world's income. That is what life is like for the "other half." These are the people who desperately need microcredit to improve their circumstances. More than a billion of them have no access to clean drinking water. More than 800 million suffer from severe hunger and malnutrition. Every hour approximately 1,200 children within this group die from preventable diseases.

These raw statistics are harrowing enough, but don't forget this: poverty is intimately personal. Remember the last time you faced a crisis. Which mattered more: how many others had the same problem or the personal impact on you and your family? Look beyond the statistics and see the people. They may be culturally different and live on the other side of the globe, but they are real human beings, people who feel joy and pain, laugh, cry, and love their children. Their poverty means much more than the statistics about how much money they do or don't have.

Poverty encompasses a long, destructive series of evils. In parts of India and China I've visited, mothers kill their infant daughters because the economics of having a baby girl can put the whole family in jeopardy. China's national one-child policy means parents want that single child to be a son to support them in old age. In India, custom dictates a girl cannot get married without a dowry, a large sum of money or other assets the girl's family must pay to the groom's family. For most of us, such situations are unimaginable, but for the majority of people in the world this is the story of their lives. For those of us who live among the wealthy few, we must make the resolute choice to confront the monster of poverty and then, as Sun Tzu advises, learn enough to conquer it.

One of poverty's most treacherous features is how its consequences compound. I suspect that is what happened to the grieving family I met in the Philippines. One day while walking through a slum built atop a garbage dump on the outskirts of Manila, I heard a commotion around one of the shanties. The crowd urged me forward to look. A young family was conducting a funeral for its baby daughter. The father sat on a small stool, staring at his feet. The mother's eyes were red and puffy from hours of crying. Yet, she thanked me repeatedly for being an outsider who noticed and cared about their heartbreak. She did not know what took her child's life. Quite possibly it was diarrhea, simple and inexpensive to cure if medication is available and affordable.

What led to this tragedy? The father could not find work, so he resorted to scavenging at a garbage dump; his family eventually had no choice but to live there. Toxicity from the decaying garbage made their child ill. The parents had no access to medical care, but probably could not have paid for medicine even if care could be found. As a result, their baby died. Rarely does poverty exist in isolation. Its crushing burden is usually a linked series of calamities that amplify one another.

Measurements of poverty typically study income or consumption levels, and those statistics are certainly useful. The whole picture, however, means getting in touch with the humanity of what it feels like to be poor, suffering, and hopeless about prospects for a better life.

The familiar designation "Third World" can be misleading, leaving the mistaken impression that only one-third, or less, of the world's population is poor. This is not the case. In fact, the moniker Third World dates back to the 1960s when it identified all parts of the world except those countries in the two Cold War power blocs: the capitalist west and communist east. Those were the "first" and "second" worlds, respectively, leaving the rest of the world, about 145 countries, as the Third World. Since then the term has become synonymous with countries ranking lowest on the United Nations' Human Development Index. In fact, the Third World could be renamed the "Two-Thirds World," which more accurately describes the proportion of people living there.

The world's wealthiest countries send foreign aid to "Two-Thirds World" nations, but the amount sent by the United States is much less than taxpayers think. The University of Maryland's Program on International Policy Attitudes conducted a poll in 2001 that found most Americans believe that 24% of the federal budget goes to overseas development assistance. Politicians, also, often leave the impression that such assistance is a major item of government spending. In reality, less than 1% of the annual U.S. government budget goes to humanitarian foreign aid. A few people have commented to me, "I don't worry about world poverty. That's why I pay taxes. It is the government's job to look after problems like that." The fact is that foreign aid, whether bilateral or multilateral, comes nowhere near meeting the need. Private giving plays a major role. Besides, my experience is that privately funded, grassroots organizations usually far outperform big government projects in terms of results they produce as measured by the cost-per-life calculation, or CPL, explained in Chapter 2.

When you think about the milestone year 2000, what comes to mind? Of course, it marked the start of a new millennium, and the much hyped Y2K bug, which proved to be a nonevent. But the year 2000 will be important for a long time for another reason. In 2000 the United Nations launched one of its most widely acclaimed initiatives ever: The Millennium Development Goals, or MDG. All 191 U.N. member nations endorsed this plan to halve the number of the people in the world living on less than $1 a day, halve the proportion of the population suffering from hunger compared to baseline statistics from 1990, and improve the lives of the world's poor in six additional ways. The aim is to reach these goals by 2015. World leaders made speeches commending the MDG and charities launched "Make Poverty History" campaigns.

Everyone's intentions were, and are, good, but, according to the *Millennium Development Goals Report 2006* published by the United Nations, the results so far are not very impressive. Parts of Asia show a strong decline in poverty, but extreme poverty in Africa remains virtually unchanged, from 44.6% of the people living on less than $1 per day in 1990 to 44% in the latest data. At the current rate of progress, 2015 could very well dawn without seeing hunger cut in half or even coming close. According to the World Bank, "Progress in eradicating hunger . . . has been slow and the situation has been worsening in some regions." It would seem that, even when the world's nations unite to fight poverty, many of the weapons are blunt. Microcredit succeeds in places where other macro efforts fail.

Levels of Poverty

In the eyes of most people, there isn't much difference between millionaires and billionaires; rich is rich. By the same reasoning, poor is poor. But, just as there are degrees of wealth, there are also levels of poverty. These levels, which have drastically different characteristics, are important because different solutions work at different levels. The 1.2 billion people who eke out an existence on $1 or less per day often exist in a perpetual state of near-starvation. Work, if any,

---

A DEADLY CHOICE

Esther, a 14-year-old African girl, faces a life-or-death decision. Her father died of AIDS, and her mother earns $1 a day working in the sweltering heat of a palm oil field. Her wages do not adequately feed her five children or pay school fees. Esther remembers how proud she had been to pass third grade, but she left school when her mother went to work. Now, however, a younger sibling is able to care for the others, so Esther expects to join her mother in the fields. Without further education she faces the same exhausting, destitute life.

But recently an older man offered to pay Esther's school fees and feed her entire family in exchange for sex. The idea makes her sick to her stomach, but she thinks it is her only way out of poverty. As for AIDS, like the rest of her village she mistakenly believes that having sex with a virgin cures AIDS. So, she reasons, if she has sex only with him, she is in no danger. Some of her friends already have relationships with older "sugar daddies." Their families have plenty to eat, and they look nice in their clean and ironed school uniforms.

Thousands of girls face a choice like Esther's. Only later do those who choose the sugar daddies become faceless statistics on AIDS mortality charts.

---

is seasonal or undependable in other ways. Moving up a level in poverty, about 1.6 billion people survive on $1 to $2 per day. They are often economically active and self-employed. Although hunger may be a constant companion, they are not likely to starve unless a significant disruption occurs, such as a breadwinner getting sick or dying, crop failure, theft, war, or natural disaster. Such a crisis would push them down a level to the utter destitution of those who live on less than $1 a day.

As you examine microcredit programs you might support, consider what poverty level the program reaches. Microcredit often works best for the poorest people. The maxim is, "The smaller the loan, the greater the impact." A program making $50 loans almost certainly reaches deeper into poverty than one dispensing $1,000 loans. Doubling an income of $1 or $2 a day is easier than doubling an income of $10 or $20 a day. By supporting a microcredit program that offers $50 and $100 loans instead of $5,000 loans, you not only reach many more people but also bring about greater change in the quality of life for the people you are helping.

We who live in wealthy countries find it hard to imagine what it would be like to never get even the smallest "break" in life. But people mired in deep poverty have no expectations of ever seeing an opportunity to advance themselves. Recently I met with people who run the largest microcredit program in the Democratic Republic of Congo, or DRC. They gave me fresh insight into why financial opportunity seems so impossibly out of reach to the average Congolese citizen. In the DRC, only one person in 1,000 has a bank account. That is why even a very small microloan seems like a miracle to all those people who are outside the formal banking system.

Women and Poverty

Often at the mercy of men who exploit them, many women are trapped in cultures that deny them education, respectable jobs, and basic human rights. Single and abandoned mothers face the same problems, exacerbated by the need to feed and care

PUTTING WOMEN AND GIRLS LAST

The Economist magazine in late 2005 detailed the extent of several patterns of gender abuse: "According to one UN estimate . . . between 113m and 200[million] women are now demographically 'missing.' This gender gap is a result of aborting of girl fetuses and infanticide in countries where boys are preferred; lack of food and medical attention that goes instead to brothers, fathers, husbands and sons; so-called 'honour killings' and dowry deaths; and other sorts of domestic violence. It implies that each year between 1.5m and 3m women and girls are lost to gender-based violence. In other words, every two to four years the world looks away from a victim count on a scale of Hitler's Holocaust.

"Women between the ages of 15 and 44 are more likely to be maimed or die from violence inflicted one way or another by their menfolk than through cancer, malaria, traffic accidents or war combined. Poor health care means that 600,000 women are lost each year to childbirth (a toll roughly equal annually to that of the Rwandan genocide)."

for their children. In some countries women are not allowed to own property. Of the 1.2 billion people who live on less than $1 a day, the majority, over 900 million, are female. The quality of life of the mother determines a child's future; yet, in every country, women are overwhelmingly poorer than men.

Poverty and Health

We cannot overstate the importance of enabling parents to provide adequate food. A 2006 report, *Repositioning Nutrition as Central to Development*, by the International Bank of Reconstruction and Development, or IBRD, a division of the World Bank, says that malnutrition damages a child irreversibly by the time that child reaches age two. The IBRD goes on to say that at least 100 million children are currently at risk of being stunted by malnutrition, yet cautions against popular feeding programs. A better response, it says, is providing nutrition education for the parents and ensuring that they can put adequate food on the table. On March 3, 2006, in its coverage of the release of the report, the *New York Times* noted, "Malnutrition is implicated in more than half of the deaths of children globally, 'a proportion unmatched by any infectious disease since the Black Death,' the bank's report says."

Thieves of Childhood

The two most frequent comments I hear from borrowers about the benefits of their loans are, "Now, I can feed my

MICROCREDIT   IN ACTION

Bintou lives in Mali, West Africa. When her husband died, she was left to raise their five children alone. Her husband owned a small goods shop, but she had no business experience. Still, she kept the store open and sold its stock. She could not, however, restock the store because funeral expenses consumed the profits. Overwhelmed and without resources, she asked her husband's former trading partners for a loan. Preying on her vulnerability, they agreed to a loan but said she must pay exorbitant interest or provide them with sexual favors. Bintou's sister helped pay off the debt, including the unreasonable interest, but in a short time Bintou was once again short of money to replenish her small inventory.

Then she heard about a new microcredit organization in her community. She talked to a project officer and was surprised to learn she qualified for a $70 microloan, enough to keep the tiny business running. The project officer helped her calculate how much of her profit to set aside for restocking, and also suggested that she add new products her customers requested. Business increased, and Bintou used additional microloans to keep up with customer demand. Her 15-year-old daughter, Fanta, is delighted with her mother's newfound hope, "Our mom used to be very sad, but [now] she pays our school fees and covers all our other food, medical, and clothing needs. And, there is joy at home."

family" and "Now, my children can go to school." Those are results to celebrate because, worldwide, 104 million children of primary school age are not able to attend school.

As difficult as poverty is for people like Bintou and her family, degradation from poverty affects millions of children in even worse ways. They are sold into slavery. Good data are difficult to collect on modern slavery since no country wants to report such unflattering statistics. Human Rights Watch has cited a possible range for child labor in India alone, "With credible estimates ranging from 60 to 115 million, India has the largest number of working children in the world." The arrangement is called by names as benign as prepaid labor or as honest as bonded slavery. Make no mistake about it. It is slavery.

My first encounter with this insidious scheme came when microcredit staff took me to visit the Kolar region of India. It had been a boom area, the place where modern gold mining began, and it is still called the golden land of India. By the time I saw it in the early 1990s, mining was at a standstill; since 2003, it has ceased completely. While there, I visited communities of Dalit families, also known as untouchables, who, because of their low caste, are not allowed to own land. They are permitted to do only menial, manual labor on farms, which is seasonal. In the off-season, they have no source of income. Land owners take advantage of this predicament by offering a lump sum advance payment for a family member to do limitless work for an entire year. Rates I encountered were $25 to $40 for a child, to no more than $100 for a strong adult. I met an Indian pastor who had coaxed a microcredit organization from Bangalore to bring microloans into the area. He insisted something had to be done because every family in the four churches he served had one or more family members captured in bonded slavery.

The year of prepaid labor is a trap. Once in it, you cannot get out, and often other family members are sucked in as well. Picture the plight of these members of the lowest caste, landless people. They do hard manual labor in the agricultural fields during the growing season, but, after the harvest, no one needs their day-labor. Soon, they become hungry and desperate. Somehow they decide which family member will become a bonded worker. Can you imagine being part of a family discussion deciding who must become a slave? The parents are needed to care for the remaining children, and, if they can stay free, they will earn more when the next day-labor season comes round. And so the lot often falls to a child, yielding enough cash so the rest of the family can eat until the planting season.

The catch is that, a year later, the bonded worker almost never goes free. One trick is to claim outrageous interest on the money advanced; another is that the worker has to pay off what is owed for food, housing, and sometimes even tools provided during the year of labor. Even apart from those tactics, the family is still back to the same problem: how to get enough money to feed everyone during the fallow season. The poor family has no choice but to renew the servitude arrangement for another year. Eventually two or three members from each family become trapped in the system and spend long days breaking rocks, working fields, weaving rugs, or hidden away as domestic servants. No one should have to live like this, least of all children, but they do. It is the harsh life of millions.

I recall telephoning my wife during that trip and telling her, "I just discovered we are buying slaves and setting them free!" This is what The Bridge Foundation, an affiliate of

Opportunity International, was doing: paying off the remaining debt a bonded worker owed and then adding on an amount to buy animals, often sheep, that the family would raise as an alternative source of income. I have seen microcredit literally free slaves.

The tragedy of modern slavery is not unique to India. Human trafficking is widespread. UNICEF estimates that 200,000 children from West and Central Africa are sold into slavery every year. Worldwide, more than a million children are trafficked annually for either prostitution or forced hard labor. While the indentured workers just described may be regarded as somewhat voluntary, trafficking of children is completely involuntary and is often accompanied by kidnapping and violence.

Slavery is not a scourge of a bygone era; it is shockingly prevalent here in the twenty-first century. Baroness Caroline Cox is one of the leading voices calling attention to modern slavery. She has great influence as former deputy speaker of the House of Lords of the British Parliament, and her credible estimate is that 27 million people are enslaved today. How tragic, considering 2007 is the bicentennial of the British Parliament outlawing slavery. What a terrible irony that, even as we celebrate how William Wilberforce and others fought for decades to abolish slavery, it is back with a vengeance.

The Vatican is calling attention to the fact that slavery today exceeds the scale of the equally immoral African slave trade of the past. In its story of November 14, 2006, the *International Herald Tribune* reported, "Human trafficking, including women forced to become prostitutes or minors forced to do child labor, is worse now than the trade in African slaves of past centuries, a top Vatican official said on Tuesday."

Gordian Knot of Poverty

In Greek mythology, the gods chose a peasant, who was on his way into town with an oxcart, to be king of Phrygia. As a sign of gratitude, he tied the wagon to a temple with a knot so complex no one could undo it. The people believed that whoever untied it would become the ruler over the entire area, which later became Asia Minor. According to legend, hundreds of years later Alexander the Great came through the place, now called Gordium, drew his sword and, in one swift stroke, slashed the Gordian knot in two.

In today's world, poverty is a Gordian knot. Its issues are complex and can seem unsolvable. Despite the best efforts of governments and charities, poverty persists. Microcredit is a sword that can split poverty's Gordian knot.

"Defeating poverty is only two words until you've looked into the face of a woman who proudly shows you her business and tells you what her family has gained as a result."

—SUSAN DAVIS

CHAPTER 9

THE BEST
DUE DILIGENCE

Phil Smith

Sitting in the Tulsa airport, I was apprehensive about my weeklong trip to Ukraine and Russia to visit two HOPE International microcredit projects. Although I had been supporting microcredit projects for two years, I had yet to meet a microentrepreneur in person. The first stop on my trip would be to visit HOPE's Ukraine organization, which had been operating for about seven years. The second would be a new project in Russia that members of my church were launching in conjunction with HOPE. It had been partly my idea, and I hoped to bring back a good report.

I had never been to this region of the world, and some childhood fears of the "Evil Empire" lingered. I did not know the language, and I dreaded dingy hotel rooms and dismal food. Above all, it was difficult leaving my family knowing that they had apprehensions, too.

On the first leg of the flight from Tulsa to Dallas-Fort Worth airport, I read *The Ultimate Gift*, by Jim Stovall. His blindness has not kept him from being a motivational speaker, prolific author, and successful businessman. Since I had been pondering how fast to spend the principal in our family's donor advised fund, two passages seemed especially appropriate:

- "Money is nothing more than a tool. It can be a force for good, a force for evil, or simply idle."
- "Assume everything is possible. Make a list of all the things you would like to do and be and have in your life. Then begin to prioritize that list as you discover the ones that generate the most passion in your soul. . . . There are no right or wrong answers, and keep in mind your dreams will grow and develop through the years."

As I read, I realized that letting money lay idle in our family's donor advised fund is a terrible waste provided we can find a better option. Although we had already put much of the fund's resources to work in microcredit, the worldwide need for capital is immense. However, I was doing new things and dreaming bigger dreams. This trip was one of them. I was taking a giant step out of my travel comfort zone to see how my microcredit ideas worked in reality.

On the next leg of the trip to Frankfurt, I set the inspirational material aside to read HOPE's operation manual for the Ukraine. It was as comprehensive as a manual for an international commercial bank and contained loan procedures, job descriptions, and human resources information. HOPE's compassion was evident in its tough love policies of not loaning money to people already in debt and ensuring that each borrower has the capability and commitment to repay a loan.

HOPE also requires that each borrower have at least two other reputable people guarantee the loan. Their knowledge of Ukrainian culture led them to offer an individual loan program rather than a group lending program. Their policies reinforced my belief that microloans must be administered by local people. Much of the information supporting the loan approval is from personal interviews, impressions of the loan officer, and the borrower's reputation, which are all impossible to assess from a desk thousands of miles away.

The next flight was to Kiev and would bring my total travel time to 22 hours. On the plane, I studied the picture of Max, HOPE's representative in Kiev, who would meet me at the airport and show me a little of the city during my six-hour layover. Max greeted me with a smile; we took a taxi to his parents' house, passing what seemed like endless blocks of dilapidated, high-rise apartment monstrosities where most of Kiev's 6 million legal and illegal inhabitants live. Forty years ago when Max's family purchased the brick, two-story home, it was in the countryside. The family continues to use every square inch of their backyard to raise vegetables and fruits. Back in the taxi, we passed apartments all the way to the city center.

Downtown Kiev looks like many other European cities with subways, buildings from the 1800s, traffic jams, and fashionably dressed people. On closer inspection, the subways are old and crowded, the buildings are crumbling, and the cars are cheap. Although people wear stylish clothes, Max said they wear the same outfit several times a week. He was especially proud to show me Independence Square, where the people had gathered in protest of the presidential election by the hundreds of thousands for the Orange Revolution that concluded in January 2005. For the previous three months there had been nationwide protests against the results of the run-off votes for president, which were popularly believed to be compromised by massive corruption and fraud. Max talked repeatedly of the risks the people had taken and how their tenacity had paid off in a new independent government and renewed hope for the future. Even a casual observation shows that the newer generation is adapting to capitalism, carrying cell phones and traveling, but the older people are having a harder time adjusting. He said that the people of Kiev are hopeful, and that for most of them, living conditions are the best in their lifetimes.

During the hour flight from Kiev to Zaporozhye my fellow passengers were Russians, Ukrainians, Asians, and Africans; not one spoke English. The departure and landing announcements were in Russian, which was disconcerting. I realized that anyone who travels outside his or her country must feel similarly disoriented.

Three of HOPE's staff members met my plane and escorted me to a hotel; I was pleasantly surprised to have a newly remodeled room on the ground floor. It was clean and comfortable, an oasis in a cement hell. The next morning I saw the city's standard apartment buildings rising above the hotel. It was difficult to tell one building from another. They all had peeling paint, broken concrete, rusty iron balconies, and laundry flapping out the windows.

I waited in the lobby to meet my guides, people who are committed to helping others engage in free enterprise with microcredit. Peter Greer, the president of HOPE, lives in Pennsylvania, but had just traveled to Ukraine by way of Moldova. He arrived with Paul Marty who moved from Minnesota with his wife to Ukraine seven years ago to start

HOPE's microcredit program. Paul oversees HOPE's programs in Ukraine, Moldova, and Russia. Andre Barkov, HOPE's program operations director in Ukraine, joined us for a breakfast of fruit pastries and rolls stuffed with sauerkraut.

Although Andre was a bit reserved at the beginning, over the next few days I found him to be fluent in many languages, well-traveled, a master of Ukrainian history and politics, and, to my delight, an expert on American and British rock-and-roll music. He also is widely read and well versed in most aspects of microcredit. I asked Andre what surprised him most about microcredit in Ukraine. He said he was surprised to find his countrymen, who had grown up under the communist system of lies, bribes, and theft, were becoming honest businesspeople who could be trusted to repay their loans.

Paul related how hard it had been to put the microcredit program in place because of governmental regulations. His persistence is one reason HOPE is the largest microcredit organization in Ukraine, the second largest country in Europe. One of his pleasant surprises was the realization that finding and training staff would be relatively easy since there were so many well-educated people available. Over the next few days, I was astounded at the quality of their organization and marveled that Paul, a former chiropractor from Minneapolis, started the program from scratch and had personally written much of the complex software. The microcredit program was in such good condition that the only pressing problem was securing enough capital to meet the vast demand for microloans.

We visited HOPE's office in the heart of Zaporozhye, a 200-year-old city of more than a million people. With four employees, it operates like a branch bank that reports to the main office in another location in Zaporozhye. A loan officer meets and interviews prospective borrowers and generates the loan applications. A loan committee evaluates the applications, and the cashier disburses loans and collects payments. One of HOPE's distinguishing characteristics is processing and approving loans quickly. Compassionate capitalism, I thought, recalling earlier days when I had waited and waited and waited for the decision on a loan that was important to me.

Later, we drove to HOPE's regional office in nearby Nikopol, which, ironically, faces a statue of Lenin and is adjacent to an ancient Scythian graveyard with worn grave markers and stone idols. Three staff members met us at the door to the office's two rooms, both freshly painted. They were eager to tell me that the office is profitable, makes 75% of its loans to women, and has an average loan size of $851. They walked us through the lending and repayment procedures, but I could barely contain my excitement about meeting some of their borrowers. For two years I had been supporting microcredit and promoting it to my friends. At last I was going to meet the microentrepreneurs who I thought and talked about so much.

We walked about six blocks to an outdoor/indoor market where many of HOPE's borrowers have their businesses. Two blocks before the market, we started seeing people on each side of the street with small amounts of goods for sale. I noticed outdated and often thoroughly worn items such as plumbing supplies, electrical appliances, and dishes. The actual market consists of tents and metal stalls that the vendors rent by the month. There were perhaps 100 vendors at this medium-sized market. With a metal stall, a vendor can lock up goods for the night, but the vendors with tents have to move their merchandise in and out every day, storing it in cars, homes, or warehouses. The vendors in the main market typically have new items such as shoes, clothes, and hardware. I learned that they travel to nearby ports or cities to buy their goods for resale. The vast majority of Ukrainians and Russians buy all of their consumer goods and food from markets such as this. Looking around the market, I was faced with the stark reality that all the vendors had to sell a certain amount of goods every week or their families might go hungry.

MICROCREDIT   IN ACTION

Vasily Bokoch is a loan officer for HOPE in Nikopol, Ukraine. He represents a seldom mentioned benefit of microcredit: the employees of microcredit organizations are among the most productive citizens of their societies. They not only have reliable incomes, but they also are a stabilizing force in their communities because of their knowledge and training. Each week, hundreds of people are influenced by their integrity, skill, and compassion. Because of Vasily's close communication with so many people, it would not be an overstatement to say that he has more influence than the loan officers at the biggest commercial banks in his city.

The microcredit program made a huge difference for these people. Most of HOPE's entrepreneurs I met had doubled or tripled their incomes through microloans. They were happy to meet us and show us their businesses. Their pride was obvious, despite my needing Andre to interpret our conversations and the dynamics of the marketplace. I met Lidia, a widow who had lost her job at a state-run factory. She sold baby clothes and had tripled her income with her series of microloans. She and her children had been barely surviving, and now she is putting them through school. I met three orphaned sisters in their twenties. With microloans, they had taken over their parents' debt-ridden dry goods business and were making a solid, reliable profit. Many others had similar stories of success. I was most struck by a woman named Irina, who was almost too busy selling pencils and notebooks to talk to us.

MICROCREDIT   IN ACTION

Irina is one of thousands who lost jobs—and with them their only source of income—at state-owned enterprises when the Ukrainian government began experiencing severe financial difficulties in the 1980s. Her son was graduating from high school, and they were desperate. He wanted to go on to college, but now they could barely afford school. She looked for a loan to start a small business, but her only option was moneylenders with interest charges of 10% a month. Her friends told her about HOPE, and she timidly applied for a loan. She used this loan to purchase pencils, paper, and other school supplies that every student needs, intending to start a school supplies business. Her business quickly increased tenfold, and she expanded it to include office supplies. She now supplies 30 businesses and delivers their orders. In addition to a store, she has eight stalls in markets around the city and employs between 8 and 12 people, depending on the season. Her business continues to grow.

Late that afternoon, we went to HOPE's main office in Zaporozhye, where we discussed plans for the proposed new microcredit program in Volgodonsk, Russia. Members of the church I attend in Tulsa wanted the incomes of some Russian pastors, church attendees, and others in the community to be increased through a microcredit program administered by HOPE. Although the project had been conceptualized a year earlier, HOPE needed to modify its successful Ukrainian model to fit the needs of a smaller community in a neighboring country. Working with complex computer models and whiteboard markers reminded me of executive sessions and board meetings in the oil business. However, rather than planning how to take over a $500 million company, we were determining the best way to make $500 microloans.

The next morning we began our 14-hour drive to Volgodonsk, Russia. We endured a two-hour border crossing and repeated police checkpoints to get through the country, but the sun setting over the Don River was a magnificent sight and worth the drive across a bridge that looked close to collapse. Rather than talking about the mishaps of communism, we discussed ways microcredit could help the country.

After a church service the next morning, we went to a cozy new restaurant for lunch with the pastor. We talked about the strategy for the microcredit program and discussed new opportunities, while I learned that it is possible to enjoy eating beef tongue. After lunch, Peter and I played basketball with some teenagers, the United States versus Russia. The United States won because Peter had been able to draft the group's best teen player for our team. A 12-year-old boy with a ragged Chicago Bulls T-shirt who was watching from the sidelines commented in broken English, "They're winning, but they're so old!" After the game we talked about what a wonderful coincidence it would be if some of those kids ended up growing businesses because of microloans that we would be making available.

ONE COMMITTED PERSON

From the 1980s through 1995, the All Souls Unitarian Church, Tulsa, Oklahoma, worked to impact human rights and justice issues in Central America, primarily by supporting direct aid groups. After years of supporting these types of projects, a seemingly endless task, the church decided to begin giving aid that could change lives for the long term. A church member, Betty Morrow, taught church leaders about microfinance, and in 1996 led them on a visit to a FINCA (Foundation for International Community Assistance) village bank in Managua, Nicaragua. The members of All Souls have since funded the establishment of 24 village banks in Nicaragua, Guatemala, Haiti, and Mexico. Betty travels thoughout the United States to inspire other churches and groups to start their own banks, carrying the message, "It only takes one committed person reaching out to others to establish lasting economic and social justice."

We were up early the next day, an exciting day. HOPE would make its first loans in Russia. The first two borrowers and their guarantors completed the paperwork, while the staff stood around them looking excited and pleased. Igor, who runs a small drugstore, received a $700 loan. Alexi, who sells hardware and gardening supplies was next. After a celebration with cake and punch, the new borrowers set off to put their loans to work while six HOPE employees and I walked through one of the local markets. From the outside it looks like a large metal box, but inside businesses grouped by type are clustered together on two floors. As we talked to one vendor, we heard how important it is to be able to differentiate oneself from other vendors by having styles for a target market. The cost of a pair of shoes was about half of that in my hometown of Tulsa. There were no designer brands but many imitations. This particular market looked more like the upscale flea market in Tulsa than the sweltering, primitive markets I had seen in many parts of Latin America.

After lunch we drove to a nearby town to see a drug and alcohol rehabilitation center run by the Volgodonsk church. Russia has a huge drug and alcohol addiction problem, and government-run agencies are few and those are generally ineffective. It was humbling to meet the residents of the center. Most had lost everything and were recovering through the center's strict discipline of work, Bible study, and separation from harmful influences. One man looked like a heavyweight boxer. He told me he had been a star athlete in school, but became addicted to drugs supplied by his best friend. Seventeen years later, he had lost his family and all his possessions. He had tried government rehabilitation programs, but he could not break his addiction until he came to the center. He has been free from drugs for two years and now helps other addicts at the center move along the road to recovery.

Somberly, I left the center wondering, "How many young people are turning to drugs every day to escape the despair of poverty?" But I knew a more useful question is, "How can we give as many young people as possible opportunities that will give them hope, instead of despair?" We visited several other markets to complete our assessment of the potential for microcredit. From what I saw and heard, the need and the market demand is vast.

Our final strategy session took place over dinner. Although the HOPE staff members are microcredit experts and have managed successful programs in several different countries, they were excited to hear some of my thoughts about debt financing and appropriate profit margins when taking inflation into account. We finished forming a business plan for the new venture in Russia that included a two-tier loan format so that we could meet the needs of people who need larger loans, and we decided how the loan program could benefit the church as well. We continued refining the plan during the four-hour car ride to Rostov-on-Don, Russia, where Peter and I began the first leg of our flight home.

Spending time with Andre and Paul gave me a much greater appreciation of the complexities of making microloans, and I realized that my attempting to give out loans directly would not be a good idea. I learned that although the concepts of microcredit apply globally, the specifics of how to provide microcredit change dramatically from country to country, and even village to village. I began to realize the importance of understanding a country's political and religious history, its past and current business practices, and its cultural differences. Microcredit organizations in Russia, which must contend with the Russian Mafia or corrupt local governments, face entirely different challenges from, for example, those in Rwanda where some loan officers can barely add or subtract. I became even more convinced that poverty has to be solved one family at a time and that these families would eventually have a noticeable, positive effect on their communities. I wondered how the age-old conflict of the haves and have-nots would come into play because of microcredit; maybe entire social and political systems would be influenced. The ripple effect of microcredit is far greater than I had ever envisioned—on both the borrowers and the lenders.

" *Doing the right thing at the right moment multiplies its effect incalculably.* "

—OS GUINNESS

CHAPTER 10

TOUGH LOVE LEADS
TO HAPPY ENDINGS

Phil Smith

William K. Warren moved from Tennessee to Oklahoma in 1916 and accepted a job as a voucher clerk for Gypsy Oil Company. From that humble beginning, he rose to the top of his industry, starting the hugely successful Warren Petroleum Company. Warren succeeded not only in business but also in philanthropy. In 1960, St. Francis Hospital in Tulsa, Oklahoma was built on the strength of the Warren family's contribution, at that time the largest gift ever given to a U.S. hospital by a single family. Tulsa lore claims that Warren monitored the construction with binoculars and quickly challenged any evidence of waste or idleness he observed. He demanded stellar performance from his company employees, and he expected no less from his charity endeavors. He made the time and exerted the effort needed to increase the performance of his philanthropy.

At a community foundation conference in Kansas City, in 2003, Eric and I were asked why people who control donor advised funds or family foundations are sometimes so reluctant to distribute money already set aside in these accounts. Many foundations spend only the minimum required by law, and some donor advised funds go years without distributing anything. To the conference attendees, this was illogical. The question resonated with me, because my own donor advised fund had been giving away only a small percentage each year. "People don't like their giving options," I answered, which was a knee-jerk response to a question I had not thought to ask of myself. I later found that indeed the majority of people don't like their giving options; they may not be able to voice what they don't like, but subconsciously they don't like their choices.

A year later, I attended a gathering of members from hundreds of wealthy families. They demand the best performance from their investments and skillfully employ every financial technique available. Many of them are generous and active philanthropists. But even though they are thoughtful about their giving decisions, they do not seem to demand nearly as much from their philanthropic investments as they do from their financial investments. In fact, just as I used to be, some appear to be unaware that they can expect and insist on strong returns from their giving. I have come to believe that this contradiction, illustrated in the graph at the top of the next page, helps fuel people's dissatisfaction with their giving options.

It does not have to be this way; it is possible to view philanthropy in the same light as investing and to expect that through microcredit you can achieve even better results than with your financial investments. Use your business skills to further your giving goals, not just the goals of a charity organ-

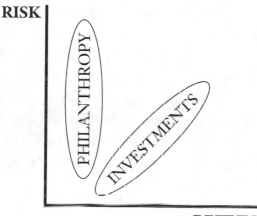

ization. Unleash the full power of your donated dollars instead of blindly dispatching your money to a general fund that may accomplish very little. Instead of letting resources snooze inside a foundation or donor advised fund, find great opportunities and put your contributions to work. I have found that my giving graph does not have to look like the one above; it can, and should, look like the one below.

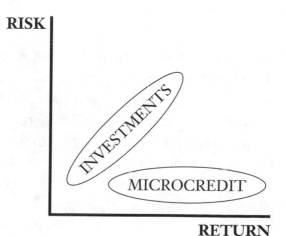

Now you know one of the two main reasons why I am a microcredit enthusiast (okay, maybe a fanatic). My giving performance puts my investment performance in the shade. My philanthropy is no longer sinking into a black hole of good intentions; it is changing an extraordinary number of lives. But there is another important reason why microcredit attracts me. It not only changes the lives of borrowers: it is changing me in good ways and having similar positive effects on others who support microcredit.

Don't Check Your Mind at the Door

Nonprofit groups frequently complain that donors check their minds at the door (although sadly, some charities encourage this) and make decisions only with their hearts. Certainly passion for humanitarian causes should be encouraged. Keep the zeal, but also keep your mind engaged to make certain you are accomplishing what you intend. If you choose to make your donations with the mind-set of an investor, here are some of the choices you might make:

- Seek charities that offer the *best return* on your investments. Though you might favor a few local charities, the location of their headquarters and the people they serve should not be the primary consideration. Instead, look for an underserved market. According to the GivingUSA Foundation, Americans contributed $260 billion in 2005, but only 2.5% of this money was allocated to international causes. Unfortunately, virtually all those who live in deep poverty live in developing countries. Despite the recognition of microfinance as a proven poverty-reduction tool, fewer than 18% of the world's poorest households have access to financial services.

- Require that the returns on your charitable investments be *measurable* and the results reported in a meaningful fashion. Unfortunately, many charities prefer to report vague anecdotes, misleading numbers, or incomprehensible financial summaries meant to convince donors that the charity operates efficiently. Since few people have the time or desire to examine their philanthropic activities under a microscope, they should demand that charities report specific measurable results. Unless results are measured, there is no good way to hold charities accountable for their actions.

- Even after intense analysis, your *investment style* should guide your decisions. Maybe you prefer a diversified portfolio to maximize return after accounting for risk. If so, you would limit your maximum investment in any single charity or cause. Maybe you are drawn to what appears to be the highest return projects, so you concentrate on one or two projects that your due diligence shows to be very effective. Whether in business or philanthropy, a successful investor has a plan and follows it. Most people invest using the modern portfolio theory of maximum return based on the level of risk undertaken and diversify their portfolios; this is simply your grandmother's advice, "Don't put all your eggs in one basket." If most of your donations currently go to one organization or cause, microcredit projects can add diversity to your portfolio and increase your overall return in terms of lives changed. At the same time, you would compare your philanthropic investments to one another and also compare them to all your giving opportunities. Using these comparisons, choose the performers that best help you achieve your philanthropic goals.

- If a charity does not meet performance expectations, move your investment elsewhere or, in other words, *adjust your portfolio*. Many financial advisers recommend selling a stock when it slips by just 7%. By using a similar strict performance measure, donors should change many of the charities they support.

- Pay *management fees commensurate with expected performance*. You might pay a hedge fund manager up to 20% of the profits, but would never pay an index fund manager on a profit basis. In mutual funds, you certainly would limit money-raising and other administrative costs to a very small percentage. Apply this principle to your philanthropy. In charities, actual administrative and fundraising costs are too often 30 to 50% of the funds raised. As an investor, outside of a brief start-up period, you would find that intolerable. Unfortunately, with many charities you may have difficulty learning the true overhead. Chapter 2 gives advice on how to penetrate fundraising materials that often paint a picture that is rosier than deserved.

In 2006, two of the world's most recognized business leaders teamed up with the goal of eradicating disease and poverty in developing countries, as well as solving other social problems. Warren Buffett pledged the majority of his estimated $44 billion fortune to the Bill and Melinda Gates Foundation. By outsourcing his philanthropy in this way, Buffett is applying the same strategy to giving away his money as he did in making it: discover and support good organizations with talented management.

"As Mr. Buffet wisely observed, philanthropy is a 'tougher game' than business. In business you try to find the easiest options, he says, but 'in philanthropy, the most important problems are those which have already resisted both intellect and money.' Moreover, whereas it is easy to tell if you are succeeding in business—you make money—in philanthropy measuring performance can be fiendishly tricky and take a lot longer. To its credit, the Gates Foundation has built performance measurements into all its projects—and importantly is prepared to axe those projects that do not come up to scratch," wrote *The Economist* magazine in July 2006.

Paying Dues or Changing Lives

Failing to look at donations as investments leads to curious outcomes. From my observations and personal experience, the majority of donations are, consciously or subconsciously, considered "dues." I frequently hear people say they feel an obligation to "give back" since society has been good to them. Both donors and charity recipients perceive that the donors are fulfilling some vague sense of obligation. Often, giving from a sense of obligation does not turn out well. Donors may have a sense of regret. Recipients of their charity may resent their ongoing dependence. Where is the joy in that? No one wants to neglect critical needs, but there are many more needs than resources, which requires a discerning approach to one's giving. Generous people face a number of difficult giving decisions. One of these is their motive for giving. Do you give thoughtfully, for results, or do you give out of habit or a sense of guilt or obligation?

Donors are often dissatisfied because of unmet expectations, thinking that recipients of our donations will be thankful. Unfortunately, we seldom receive this affirmation because recipients can also see much of our giving as our obligation. Donors' expectations of gratitude are not met, which causes frustration, rather than joy. The more dues we pay, the more frustrated we become. To increase our joy, we need to change our expectations and give with an investment mentality, not a charity mind-set. The surprising result will be that the most good occurs for the least cost.

My giving history reflects that of many of my friends. My family has primarily supported churches and local charities without comparing their effectiveness to other alternatives. As an example, my hometown of Tulsa has a relatively small population of homeless people. However, there are a large number of active, vocal, and influential people who are dedicated to meeting the needs of these unsheltered people. The city has many excellent services for temporary shelter, food, and guidance to other social services. The people involved in this effort are extraordinarily dedicated to their endless task. As you can imagine, it was easy for our family to join this worthwhile effort. Yet, although the community spends many thousands of dollars a year per homeless person, only a small percentage of these people move to permanent homes or find solutions to their problems. I do not deny that these people are in need or that their suffering can be alleviated, but I also cannot deny the fact that hundreds of people in other countries could move

MICROCREDIT IN ACTION

In 1990, Jeff Rutt would have been an unlikely choice to become one of microcredit's major players. At the time, he and his wife were working 14-hour days as dairy farmers in Lancaster County, Pennsylvania. Jeff wanted a change and decided to try real estate. Initially he experimented with a few small remodeling jobs. He went on to become a major developer, founding Keystone Custom Homes, named America's Best Builder three times by Builder Magazine. *When Jeff's church decided to partner with a "sister church" in Ukraine, he got involved. During a visit to Ukraine, Jeff discovered that the sister church members did not want charity; they wanted jobs so they could support their families and their church. After a few early missteps while trying to help, Jeff founded HOPE International to provide microloans and to start afternoon Bible clubs for children. In just a few years, HOPE was making microloans throughout Ukraine and in 12 other countries. Jeff is so enthusiastic about microcredit that he donates the profits from several houses each year to make microcredit loans, and he has inspired other independent builders to do the same. Like many people who are both successful and significant, Jeff is even more inspired by his philanthropy than by his thriving business.*

out of poverty permanently for the cost of helping just one homeless person in Tulsa. So, although I still use my donor advised fund to help causes such as the homeless in Tulsa, I have shifted a significant percentage of giving away from these kinds of activities.

When investment skills are applied to charitable decisions, the transaction takes on a new, wiser character. The donor and recipient become partners who agree to meet certain obligations so that the return for both is higher. Investment philanthropy produces strong positive feelings in givers and the person invested in feels like a valued partner, not a charity case. Whether homeless in Tulsa or hungry in Zimbabwe, my bottom line is the cost-per-life changed (CPL), not the tragedy. As CNN's Anderson Cooper put it, "There should be no sliding scale of sorrow."

The Missing Piece

Jeff Rutt's journey is not unique. Microcredit organizations around the world are populated with people like him. You may wonder why these people are so passionate about microcredit. Talking to them, you see a spark in their eyes and purposeful energy in their actions. It is a spark that seems to permeate the lives of everyone associated with microcredit.

I have often pictured my life as a jigsaw puzzle. Education, marriage, children, and my faith are the important edge pieces that frame my life. Fortunately for me, those quickly fell into place. Rapid career advancement and outside interests were easy pieces with obvious patterns and colors. Then came those long times of bewilderment. Many pieces should have fit somewhere, but would not snap into place. A number of pieces seemed to be missing. And, some pieces that had been jammed into place with confidence began to look like pieces of someone else's puzzle. For a person like me who found answers in spreadsheets and databases, a jigsaw-puzzle life was unsettling. As I struggled to keep intact the pieces of a career, a family, and a spiritual center, two irritating pieces, which should have fit together seamlessly, refused to align.

The two pieces were generosity and joy. Why did the generosity that my grandparents and parents instilled in me not produce more joy? Worse, I saw the same disconnect in many other generous people. What happened to "It is more blessed to give than receive?" Did the biblical proverb not apply in a postmodern world?

Messages of the Mentors

Becoming a contemporary Diogenes, with a laptop instead of a lamp, I started traveling to find mentors who could tell me the truth about giving. My quest eventually led me around the nation; but it started in my hometown with a legendary oil man, George Kaiser, who has been a friend for nearly 30 years.

George is a self-made multibillionaire considered by many to be the epitome of intelligence and generosity. By his nature and actions, he mentors hundreds of people in their business and philanthropic decisions. During a meeting in 1996, George and I talked about the needs of people in our community and around the world. His parting comment was, "Phil, the more you want to help people, the more money it takes. You should go make more money." I took on the challenge and started another business.

A HAND UP FOR HAITI

In the mid-1990s, Anne Hastings was a successful management consultant in Washington, D.C. She decided to invest her talent in parts of the world where people are struggling. Her first plan was to join the Peace Corps, but instead, she was directed to a priest in Haiti doing some amazing work. Shortly thereafter, Anne joined with Father Joseph Philippe to grow a microcredit organization for the benefit of the poorest people in Haiti. She promised him one year. After ten years Anne has no plans to leave Haiti, or her beloved Fonkoze.

Fonkoze, a Haitian Creole acronym for *Fondasyon Kole Zepòl*, which means, "The Shoulder-to-Shoulder Foundation," is the largest microfinance organization in Haiti, offering a range of financial services to the rural-based poor. It has more than 90,000 depositors, more than 30,000 active borrowers (97% of whom are women), and 26 branch offices throughout the island. Unusually, Fonkoze's capital structure and income are built on the savings of its extremely poor clients and the money that is transferred to them from Haitian relatives living overseas.

Six years later, when we visited again, George said, "Now, you have to learn the very best ways to help people. It's harder than you think. And, find something to pursue with passion." He wrote out a list of people to meet and ideas to consider. He also prompted me to set up a donor advised fund in the Tulsa Community Foundation that George and other prominent citizens of Tulsa had founded (which grew to be the largest community foundation in America in just eight years). I headed off on my quest to find the activity that would be meaningful to others and kindle a strong passion in me.

It was a humbling experience to learn that the world is full of compassionate, generous people who are willing to share their experiences. This book is not long enough to talk about all the people who shared with me, but here are a few of their thoughts:

- If you want to give more, you need to have more to give.
- No matter how much you already give, you can reduce your expenses and give more.
- Innovation is a key to improving the lives of others. With skill, imagination, and relentless pursuit, effective new solutions can be found.
- Cooperating with others multiplies resources for everyone. Finding and using the right contacts and advisers improves everyone's position.
- If you give out of guilt or obligation, you will miss the joy of giving.

Even my mother moved me along in my quest to find effective ways to give by handing me the book *Don't Just Give It Away*, by Renata J. Rafferty. In the beginning of the book, the author talks about observing a lack of joy in donors,

"Ironically, many of the individuals least satisfied by their charitable giving are among the most prominent, visible, and generous financial contributors to nonprofits within their communities." She notes that philanthropy is a state of mind—not just the act of giving away immense amounts of money. She writes that philanthropists are "optimistic, determined, energized, and creative . . . entrepreneurial . . . . Philanthropy is a calculated investment made with the expectation that humankind—or some small part of it—will be profoundly, measurably, and often permanently changed for the better as a direct result of the contribution." Philanthropists know that the wiser the gift decisions, the more effective the results. They have a plan and a vision for going beyond the ordinary. They evaluate the extent of the need and the cost-efficiency of the different players who work in the same cause. They demand accountability. By focusing on fewer organizations, they develop relationships with people within the organizations and often the beneficiaries. They say "no" without guilt and "yes" without pride.

Yet, even as I tried to follow all of my mentors' ideas and do a good job of giving, my quest for passion was unfulfilled. I faithfully did my duty and checked off obligations like items from a grocery list. Then I noticed something curious. Even many of the incredibly generous givers I have known often seemed to have the same problem of fitting together those two pieces: generosity and joy. Then, my quest took a different turn.

Adequately describing Steven Dow would be impossible. As a champion for the poor in Tulsa, he is Superman, Robin Hood, and Albert Einstein all in one. He gave up a promising

A CHILD OF MICROCREDIT

Dumas Siméus thunders from the podium like an ancient prophet, but his message is for today's audience. He is the eldest of 12 children who grew up in the depths of poverty in Haiti. With tears in his eyes, he talks about following his mother from city to city as she bought and sold any available item to make enough money to feed her family. He tells how microcredit gave her the advantage she needed to grow her business and send him to school. He gives kudos to microcredit and education for his degrees from Howard University and the University of Chicago, and for his building of Siméus Foods International, one of the largest processors of frozen foods for restaurants and institutional customers. As Dumas finishes his talk, he urges the audience to remember that the next child they help with microcredit might find a cure for cancer, solve an international dispute, or provide jobs for hundreds of people. The possibilities are endless, he says, only if poverty can be defeated.

law career to work more than full time on behalf of the underprivileged in Tulsa. His hard work and intellect have produced improvements in low-income housing, tax reform, and education and have provided many other benefits for tens of thousands of people. I met with Steven after he had taken a vacation to the Caribbean—and had looked beyond the attractions noted in guidebooks. He had seen how the island people really live. This protector of Tulsa's poor was visibly affected by what he had seen and experienced on his trip. I left his office with a new piece for my puzzle, one that changed the picture: because of governmental safety nets, the poor in developed countries are well off when compared to the poor in developing countries. So the search to find my passion was not going to end in poor neighborhoods in the United States, but in remote villages and slums in countries that I previously could not have found on a map.

The Microcredit Puzzle

As with my life, learning about microcredit has also been like putting together a jigsaw puzzle. Surprisingly, the last piece in the microcredit puzzle proved to be a critical piece in my life puzzle. For microcredit, the easy pieces along the edges are the stories of people whose lives have been changed. The stories are thrilling and easy to understand. Once capital becomes available, their business and personal improvements seem logical. It takes only a little loan, not a gift. The big colorful middle pieces also slipped easily into place, the financial power of microcredit with its levers and financial engineering. But this again brought me to the long, and by now familiar, period of puzzlement. Why are people involved with providing microcredit so crazed about it? Why are people who could make a lot of money in business dedicating their lives to 12-hour workdays for low salaries with microcredit organizations?

- Why did Peter Greer work in Rwanda and later become president of HOPE International instead of something more lucrative that he could have done with his graduate degree from Harvard?
- Why did Alex Counts with an economics degree from Cornell and a Fulbright scholarship, move to Bangladesh to learn about microcredit before heading Gramcen Foundation?
- Why did Louise Makau Velle move from Kenya to Paris to earn her undergraduate degree, continue on to the United States to earn her master's degree, and then use her education to focus on microcredit and other projects in Africa through Geneva Global?

As I talked to many people involved with microcredit organizations, I found a common thread: they had joy! And I wanted that joy. It took me some time to fathom the reasons for this difference between the people involved with microcredit and most of the other dedicated givers and workers in nonprofits I have known. It was not their degree of passion, dedication, or hard work. Those are strong, of course. There is more to this dynamic. I am sure that there are many other reasons I have yet to learn, but one stands out. It begins with a lesson not taught in school.

The most satisfying equation in the world is $1 + 1 = 3$. The most satisfying business relationship is two partners creating more value than they could separately. The most satisfying personal relationship is two people creating a powerful union. The best ideas come from joining two independent pieces of information and discovering an unexpected positive conclusion.

Through microcredit, donors, borrowers, and microcredit staff all become partners in solving complex problems and meeting a shared goal. Donors provide money for microloans, and microcredit organization employees administer the loans. Borrowers increase their incomes and pay back the loans. Unlike a charity or grant, these relationships are reciprocal, rich with mutual trust. Victories are won together rather than fought in separate, ongoing battles. These partners do not labor day after day just to meet temporary needs. They permanently change lives. I found how joy and generosity can come together to enrich the lives of everyone involved.

The needs of people around the world are massive, but usual solutions are ephemeral and often excessively expensive. In contrast, people working with microcredit see real progress every day. They see borrower after borrower improve their lives permanently. They watch the future change for children, women, and men as poverty and poverty-related problems are solved with remarkably tiny amounts of money.

The Next Step Is Yours

You now know what Pam and Pierre Omidyar, Eric and I, and tens of thousands of other givers have discovered about microcredit. How it defeats the cycle of poverty and its related scourges for vast numbers of people, one family at a time. Why it is so powerful and effective from a financial standpoint. How it can give you satisfaction and joy.

About the only limit to the growth of microcredit and the resulting triumph over poverty is the lack of funding for more microloans. How far this superb solution can reach rests to a large extent in the bank accounts, foundations, and donor advised funds of potential supporters. We have the ability to help billions of the world's poor bootstrap themselves out of poverty, not with charity, but with the partnership of microcredit.

I have made my choice and am investing all three Ts: my time, talent, and treasure. My personal dream, which is within reach, is to enable at least a million people to raise themselves out of poverty. Realizing that dream will be one of the finest accomplishments of my life. Please join me so that, together, we can help billions of the world's poorest people become self-sufficient and live with dignity.

QUESTIONS AND ANSWERS

Terry, a physician and businessman, has visited with Phil to discuss the subject of microcredit over the past year. When he had the opportunity to corner Phil and Eric at the same time, he seized the chance to ask several probing questions. Since Terry helps many other physicians both invest and make charitable donations, he wanted to make sure that he understood microcredit well enough to explain it to them.

Terry: *Phil's enthusiasm for microcredit has me convinced that it is the best solution for poverty-related problems. But, even the most powerful medicines have limitations. What are some of microcredit's limitations?*

Eric: The United Nations estimates that 4 billion people live on less than $4 per day. I believe that microcredit could help the vast majority of those people. Sometimes I hear people say they "only want to give loans to the very poorest of the poor." I am enthusiastic about reaching as deep as possible into poverty, but who are the "poorest of the poor?" Actually, the very poorest people are those near death, extremely ill, severely handicapped, young abandoned children, and discarded elderly. These people are not candidates for microloans. Neither are the nomadic tribes that I have encountered in West Africa. I doubt that microcredit would be able to help them, and if it could, servicing those loans would be quite a challenge. Then, of course, poverty is worsened every day by war, natural disaster, and economic chaos. Sometimes interventions other than microcredit are needed first in those situations to lay the groundwork so microcredit can help at a later time.

Terry: *I'm leery of creating dependency with my donations. There's no dignity in that, not for me and not for the people I wish to help.*

Eric: Creating dependency is a troublesome risk for most charities and governments. One of the powerful aspects of microcredit is that these are loans, not gifts. This appeals to many people in poverty, because handouts make them feel diminished. I recall repeated instances when people have proudly looked me in the eye and said, "I paid back my loan." There is dignity in that. People instinctively know that a receiver relinquishes power to the giver, whether the giver is trying to get something back or not. That is why charity is often as resented as it is appreciated.

Phil: And I have both heard and seen with my own eyes that people who receive microloans almost always express more joy and appreciation when they repay their loans than when they receive them. Honoring a debt is a sign of independence and personal accomplishment.

Terry: *From what you've told me, microcredit works well in developing countries. Does it work in developed countries like Australia, Japan, England, or the United States?*

Phil: For the borrowers, yes; for the lenders, not so well. Microcredit programs in developed countries struggle to be self-sustaining because administration costs are high, loan sizes are large, and borrowers are reluctant to cross-guarantee the loans of fellow borrowers.

Eric: Having seen the return on investment on domestic microcredit programs and their limited success, I prefer to recommend programs in developing countries.

Terry: *It is difficult to focus on needs a world away. I see so many needs right here in Tulsa.*

Phil: Four years ago, location dictated how empathetic I was to someone's plight. I conformed to the pattern of many people who have about the same amount of empathy for the deaths of 50,000 people in a faraway country as for 50 people on the other side of their own country or for the death of one child in their own neighborhood. It has been a difficult shift for me to make, but I now try to have equal empathy for all people, no matter where they live.

Eric: Phil knows that money can be used much more pow-
erfully in developing countries and that a life in
another country is as valuable as a life in his own
neighborhood. It's difficult to look beyond local
needs, but think in terms of social safety nets.
Suffering people in wealthy countries have government aid programs and a host of private charities to
turn to. In many parts of the world, there are no social
safety nets. The needs are much greater.

Terry: *I was surprised when you told me that most microcredit
organizations charge high interest rates. How can this be in
the best interests of the borrowers?*

Eric: The most important issue for the borrower is having
access to credit. If the organization does not charge a
high-enough interest rate, it will go out of business,
which is highly detrimental to both the borrower and
the community. What may seem like high interest
rates are necessary to cover the administrative costs of
small loans made at locations near the borrowers.

Terry: *How do microcredit organizations function when interest
charges are prohibited by law, cultural mores, or religious
beliefs?*

Eric: They can charge legally permissible fees or commis-
sions and may charge for other services like training
that are provided along with the loans.

Phil: The services are geared to helping the borrower succeed in business. Sometimes all that stands between

success and failure is an understanding of inventory control and competitive pricing. The price of a seminar or workshop is recouped in increased profits. If the local officials are supportive of helping the people in their community, a way can be found.

Terry: *Inflation or hyperinflation must cause problems for the lending program and the borrower.*

Phil: Yes it does. In fact, the higher the inflation rate, the greater the problems. At a minimum, the interest rate charged to borrowers has to be high enough to overcome inflation or the organization cannot sustain itself. Just as in developed countries, inflation is an incentive to spend and not to save. Inflation destroys the value of savings, which is one of the assets that borrowers are encouraged or even required to have.

Eric: This is an example of the hardships people in the developing world face that are unimaginable to those of us who live in wealthy countries. When I became CEO of Opportunity International, our partner in Peru was facing inflation of more than 7,000%! Then, as we set up lending programs in Russia and Eastern Europe, some of those countries hit spikes of 1,000 to 2,000% inflation. Amazingly, it is possible to survive in situations with such high inflation rates, but very, very difficult. In some places, the program officers had to adjust interest rates daily and meet with borrowers daily to help them reset their prices. Hyperinflation is a terrible stress on both the people and the microcredit programs. It is possible to minimize the damage, but runaway inflation will always do harm. This is why microcredit organizations must be careful when borrowing in a major foreign currency while lending and collecting in local currency. If the organization is borrowing hard currency but operating strictly in local currency, sophisticated management is needed to keep the values in balance. Some organizations have that competency. Others do not. That is an important point of due diligence if you are thinking of loaning money to a microcredit group to lend to its clients.

Terry: *You keep saying "micro," but I'm not sure what that means in currency. What's the maximum amount of a microloan?*

Eric: Loan sizes vary from country to country and even from organization to organization. At some point microloans become big enough that they should be called small-business loans. A relatively large microloan could be $200 in Rwanda and around $5,000 in Russia. Keep in mind that as loans grow larger, the number of people served grows smaller. If you're looking to see the maximum number of lives changed with your donation, you would be more satisfied with a program in Rwanda than one in Russia.

Terry: *I don't like putting my charitable contributions into a sinking black hole, and it sounds like microcredit programs have the potential to become self-sustaining. Yet, how can a charity be sustainable?*

Phil: Before I answer your question, let's make sure that we agree on the definition of sustainable. Some organizations believe sustainable means that a program's interest and fees exceed its administrative costs (overhead plus operating expenses) and bad debts. Other organizations believe that annual donations should be counted as income, while a few argue that inflation should be added to the cost side. To be truly sustainable over a long period of time, a program must collect enough interest and fees to cover administration costs, bad debts, and inflation. If the organization is borrowing some of the funds it uses to lend, then that interest cost must be added to the sustainability calculation as well.

Eric: There are several highly technical formulas to compute the sustainability of microcredit organizations that are important to know if you are running a program or if you are considering investing heavily in microcredit. Before putting a large amount of money into a program, you may want an independent adviser to calculate sustainability for you. But don't let these complex computations obscure the simplicity of the concept. You want to know the answer to a common-sense question, "If you and other supporters stop providing new money, what happens?" Over the following few years, would the value of the loan portfolio hold up or shrink because some of the money would be needed to pay operating costs? If the lending program can maintain the value of its portfolio and keep serving the same number of people without new cash infusions, then it is sustainable.

Terry: *OK, why are you such a fanatic about sustainability?*

Phil: Terry, do you remember your first attraction to microloans? It fascinated you that after one borrower paid back a loan, another poor family got to use the same amount of money. That's the great power of microcredit. The same money is used over and over. However, if a program is not sustainable, some of that power is lost.

As an example, if a program's income exactly equals its total expenses, then it is breaking even or barely sustainable. If a program's income is less than its expenses, then it is not sustainable. In practical terms, that means when a loan is paid back, not all of the money will be available to loan to someone else. The loan pool is shrinking. This greatly impacts lending programs. A program that is slightly above mere sustainability will build its loan portfolio and be able to help a lot more people. One that is far less than sustainable is in danger of running out of money after a few years. Let's see what happens when an initial loan of $100 is repaid and loaned to other poor families. After 20 loan cycles, see the difference in the total amounts loaned depending on what percentage of that $100 is available for the next loan.

% of Reloan	Total Amount Loaned in 20 Cycles
110	$5700
100	$2000
90	$ 900
80	$ 500

As you can see, the amount available for reloaning has an exponential effect on the total amount of loans eventually made. It is a huge advantage for a program to be sustainable or profitable, and a huge disadvantage for it to be less than sustainable.

Terry: *Then why wouldn't I want to support only sustainable programs?*

Eric: There are several good reasons. First, a program might be new and not have had time to become sustainable. Second, by giving a program more capital you might make it sustainable. Third, a program might be providing other important services along with microcredit. Think about a lending program that is just sustainable, right at breakeven, but also delivers medical services. If all of the costs are combined into a single program figure, it would look unsustainable because of the added services. The more medical services provided, the worse the program will look if sustainability is the only metric. This is why Microcredit Plus programs need thoughtful evaluation. If you value those extra services as a donor, think of your donations as partly going to a sustainable microcredit program and partly going to subsidize other services, which are probably provided at a very advantageous cost.

Terry: *I certainly wouldn't mind subsidizing services that I value, especially if they are provided at a much lower cost because the microcredit organization provides an efficient way to deliver services. However, I don't want to subsidize overhead for some parent organization.*

Eric: You can avoid that if you specify that your donations must go directly to a specific loan portfolio. However, that stance may be a little unreasonable. If you want to use an international organization, it has overhead costs that someone has to pay. It is reasonable for you to pay a modest amount for its service. Keep in mind that it is not only fundraising but often providing valuable technical assistance such as training, supervision, and program audits. One of your jobs as an intelligent donor is to determine which entities can meet your goals while having reasonable overhead expenses. You can avoid some of those costs by going directly to a local microcredit provider in a less developed country, but your expenses and risks may increase in other ways. Efficiency, which I calculate as the cost to change one life, the cost-per-life or CPL, is one important measure. Quality of programs is another. Keep those two factors in a reasonable balance.

Terry: *Does microcredit work for churches and missions programs?*

Phil: Many church programs struggle financially because they don't address the poverty of their members. Providing a way for people to progress both in their faith and economic well-being helps everyone. Church members prosper, and the local churches have larger offerings. This does not automatically mean churches should rush out and start lending programs. It works best when groups doing spiritual ministry partner with local microcredit organizations rather than trying to make microloans directly. Imagine a preacher or a group of elders making loan decisions without having to answer questions of favoritism. It's best to avoid any risk of controversy.

Eric: Besides, when people are extremely poor, all their energy and attention must be devoted to mere survival. Abraham Maslow's famous hierarchy of needs describes that. Africans have a more colorful way of expressing the same thought with a popular saying, "Empty bellies have no ears." It is very difficult for people to appreciate the love of God when they are malnourished.

Terry: *Given the great need for microloans, this may seem like a naïve question, but I'm wondering if microcredit organizations ever compete with one another.*

Eric: This happens occasionally, but most organizations try to meet underserved needs in underserved locations. So it is fairly rare to find multiple lending programs in the same community. I am not as concerned about competition as I am by another problem that exists when more than one microcredit organization operates in a given community. Just as relatively poor people in wealthy countries can get into trouble by juggling credit card debt, paying off one card with another, something similar can happen on a smaller scale with microloans. When this occurs, someone may take out a loan with one organization to cover repayment of a loan from a competing organization. This does not improve lives and is certainly not something the microcredit organizations want. Your question is a good one to include when doing due diligence on a program you may want to support. Ask about other lending programs working in the same community.

Terry: *Does microcredit work better in cities or rural areas?*

Phil: Another powerful feature of microcredit is that it works well in both rural and urban areas. A microcredit provider must decide what populations it can efficiently and effectively serve. This decision affects the program structure and the services. There is no right or wrong, no greater need in the cities than in the countryside, just a choice to be made.

Eric: Urban lending programs are more popular. It is easy to see why. Distances are shorter, and populations are more compact in urban areas. Each loan officer can work with more borrowers, which makes transactions cheaper, though office and labor costs may be higher. There are other trade-offs. Literacy is often higher in cities, but rural people tend to be more loyal and connected to one another. One of the biggest differences is that rural lending involves agriculture. Farming can mean higher risks because of weather, crop disease, and fluctuating market prices. Microloans work best in situations where the borrower has some control over profit margins. But just because it is easier to manage loans in cities does not mean that is where all programs should operate. Much of the worst and least addressed poverty is among farmers.

Terry: *Could a foundation make microloans as part of program related investments (PRIs)?*

Phil: Absolutely. A common way would be for a foundation to loan money to a microcredit organization at a low interest rate for a specific amount of time. This transaction would be beneficial to both parties.

Terry: *How can I have closer involvement with projects I decide to support?*

Eric: That is a good subject for discussion with leaders of any group you may want to support. Their response may inform your decision making. Almost any group will provide regular reports about its lending program. It will welcome you if you want to visit and see the program firsthand. Depending on your professional skills, you may have something to offer either in the field or with the organization's support office in your home country.

Other kinds of charitable groups such as schools, museums, or hospitals have predictable ways volunteers can help. Microcredit is not like that. Lending organizations rarely have many volunteers. When they do, however, they are often highly prized relationships. The key word is *fit*. When there is a good match between a volunteer's skills and ways the organization can use them, it is enormously satisfying to both parties.

Terry: *So I can visit microcredit projects?*

Phil: Yes, if you are willing to travel. Most microcredit organizations welcome visits to their projects, and field staff and borrowers are encouraged by your interest. My trip to Ukraine was out of my travel comfort zone, but it turned out to be the most inspiring trip of my life.

Eric: Many organizations have regular trips just for donors and will make all of the arrangements for you, including sightseeing. Most are willing to assist you if you prefer to go on your own, rather than as part of a group tour. Taking supporters and potential funders to visit overseas projects was one of the highlights of my work with microcredit organizations.

Terry: *I'm interested in microcredit, even more now that I have seen your enthusiasm, but I'm also interested in helping to solve other global problems. How can I ignore the fact that AIDS is wiping out an entire continent?*

Phil: Microcredit is like a broad-spectrum antibiotic. When people work their way out of poverty, a host of other tragedies improve as well. We can direct you to a microcredit program that addresses any specific problem you are most drawn to solving. Microcredit groups often run parallel programs that fight disease, provide education and vocational training, preserve the environment, empower women, and help war orphans, AIDS orphans, and other vulnerable children; the list goes on. Through microcredit you can solve or alleviate many problems with the fewest possible dollars.

Terry: *Shouldn't my church, the United Way, and the government be taking care of these problems by using my contributions and tax payments?*

Eric: Microcredit is not the priority intervention method for any of those groups. Churches, governments, and fundraising organizations all support microcredit programs, but these programs are usually a very small part of their overall activities. Private donations are still a very big factor in the growth of microcredit. Keep in mind also that most microcredit organizations are specialists. Lending is more complex than running many other kinds of social services, like feeding programs. Microcredit is essentially running a bank for poor people. The way it is supported and the way it operates are unlike other charitable activities.

Terry: *I have this uneasy feeling that the microcredit process looks good on paper, but the results may not be as good as advertised.*

Phil: Like every other cause, enthusiastic advocates can overpromise and underperform. In addition, there are always a few people who reduce efficiency through inexperience and a very few who criminally divert funds to their own interests. I advise people to work with excellent organizations if they want minimum involvement and to take extra precautions when working with a new project.

Terry: *Do you think that microcredit is just a fad, the flavor of the day in the relief and development world?*

Phil: Not at all. The effectiveness of microcredit has proven its long-term value. Further, it should continue to grow as donors find it to be a superior method of solving poverty issues. Interestingly, even if donors develop "fatigue," many good programs are or will become self-sustaining, able to keep making microloans without ongoing support from the outside.

Eric: We're back to the subject of sustainability, aren't we? Even if the world turns to another poverty intervention with great enthusiasm—though I cannot imagine what that would be—microcredit programs will endure.

Terry: *Okay, you guys have covered all my questions. Where can I sign up?*

Phil: There is a really good book recently written about microcredit titled *A Billion Bootstraps*. Look in Chapter 7 and in the Appendixes for some excellent sources to help you get started. In fact, I wouldn't be surprised if one of your friends hands you an autographed copy of that book very soon.

A VERY BRIEF HISTORY OF MICROCREDIT

As far back as the year 1515, Pope Leo X issued a ruling in favor of organizations called *montes pietatis*, or "mounts of piety," declaring that lending to the poor is an act of mercy. These groups asked only nominal collateral from their borrowers, as opposed to those we would today call loan sharks. So we have evidence that small loans to help poor people existed long before the 1970s, when some would say the concept was invented.

Microcredit in its modern form was developed nearly simultaneously by the founders of three well-known microcredit organizations: ACCION International, Opportunity International, and Grameen Bank. Founded in 1961 to address poverty issues in Latin America, ACCION began making loans to microbusinesses in Brazil in the early 1970s. In its first four years, the organization provided 885 loans, helping to create or stabilize nearly 1,400 jobs. It is now one of the largest microcredit providers throughout Latin

America, the Caribbean, and Africa. Also in the early 1970s, an American working in Latin America and an Australian working in Indonesia started microcredit programs that merged to become Opportunity International. In late 2006, Opportunity International was serving poor people in more than 30 countries by working through affiliates to provide microloans, basic business training, and counsel.

Grameen Bank is the most documented microcredit pioneer and has the greatest worldwide name recognition. In 1974 after a famine caused massive starvation in Bangladesh, Professor Muhammad Yunus, an economist, experimented with ways to help people in Bangladesh lift themselves from poverty. He found that lending small sums of money so people could start their own businesses was a sustainable solution to hunger and poverty. In 1976, he founded Grameen Bank, now one of the largest microfinance institutions in the world, which by 2006 had served more than 6 million poor families with microloans, savings, insurance and other services. As of September 2006, the bank was 94% owned by its clients, the other 6% belonging to the government of Bangladesh. Grameen Bank's methods have been replicated around the world more often than any other microfinance model.

Dr. Yunus and Grameen Bank were awarded the 2006 Nobel Peace Prize, which catapulted microcredit into the mainstream of public awareness. In its citation in Oslo, Norway, the Nobel Committee said, "Lasting peace cannot be achieved unless large population groups find ways in which to break out of poverty. Microcredit is one such means. Development from below also serves to advance democracy and human rights."

In the early days of microcredit, lending money to poor people instead of shipping in food and clothing was a radical idea and not easily accepted by traditional charities or donors. Skeptics could not imagine that poor people would pay back loans. Years of experience and millions of loans later, the data show that poor people are good credit risks with better repayment rates than people who live in rich countries.

Eventually the idea of small loans as a form of self-help for poor people caught on. Microcredit began winning the imagination of charities and farsighted donors. In the process, this new wave of popularity had the unintended by-product of hurting microcredit's credibility. New microcredit enthusiasts stampeded to the developing world and set up lending programs. Many were ill prepared, not well grounded in microcredit methods, and not adequately capitalized. As in any boom cycle, there were plenty of failures along with the many successes. By the mid-1980s, many microcredit organizations were being criticized because of their high loan default rates and other deficiencies. These uneven results, along with deserved and undeserved negative publicity, created a backlash from private and government funders.

Despite the industry's missteps, its successes were undeniable. The microcredit programs that survived were sharpened by experience and began incorporating new tools, practices, and strategies increasing impact and reducing risk for both their programs and borrowers. Emphasis changed from rapidly disbursing loans to building sustainable programs.

Around the year 2000 many of the larger microcredit organizations made a decided shift in favor of setting up formal financial institutions. These institutions began attracting government funding and learned to manage borrowed capital to build their portfolios instead of relying exclusively on charitable donations to replenish overhead costs, portfolio losses, and loan expansion.

Since each microcredit organization has different goals and tactics, it is impossible to summarize the full scope of the status of microcredit in 2006. The Microcredit Summit Campaign—www.microcreditsummit.org—and others are working to consolidate worldwide data on the microcredit movement. This much is certain. About four out of five microloans are made to women; microcredit organizations are trying hard to access government and commercial funding sources; microcredit experts want to reach more of the very poor rather than segments of the population that are only marginally poor. Pressure, however, is building from funding sources to get excellent financial results, which will drive loans toward city dwellers and those who are comparatively less poor. Microcredit has gone through continual evolution since the early 1970s, and it appears that the pace of its development is accelerating with the influx of larger numbers of experienced business people.

SELECTED MICROCREDIT ORGANIZATIONS

Microcredit Funds

MicroCredit Solutions Fund
(www.genevaglobal.com or +1-866-743-6382)

In 2005, Geneva Global formed the multimillion dollar Micro-
Credit Solutions Fund so donors could support microloans
quickly and efficiently. The pooling of donor funds allows
donors of even modest amounts to participate in unique
microcredit opportunities, while larger donors may designate
their funds to specific microcredit projects within the fund.
The fund benefits from Geneva Global's worldwide access to
projects and its professional research and oversight.

Microcredit Clearinghouse
(www.microcreditclearinghouse.org)

The Microcredit Clearinghouse maintains descriptions of
approximately 50 excellent microcredit-related projects avail-

able through various microcredit organizations. It was formed to find philanthropic opportunities for foundations and individuals willing to share information they gather. Anyone desiring to fund projects costing more than $250,000 may access this restricted Web site to obtain specific information.

Microcredit Providers

More than 3,000 microcredit providers are working in nearly every corner of the world, from remote villages to urban slums. This list is a sample of the variety of organizations and not an endorsement of any of them. Lesser known grassroots organizations may be even more efficient than some of the large groups listed below. Other microcredit providers may be found by using the resources listed in Appendix C.

ACCION International
(www.accion.org or +1-617-625-7080)
This is one of the largest microcredit providers in Latin America, the Caribbean, the United States, and parts of Africa, with partners in 22 countries. ACCION offers group lending as well as individual loan programs. It was one of the first to set up a formal bank to make loans to poor people rather than lending through a nonprofit service organization. Creating formal financial institutions is now a major trend in the microcredit movement.

ASA
(www.asabd.org)
Started in 1978 to provide microloans in Bangladesh and technical assistance to microloan organizations in other countries,

ASA has more than 2 million borrowers who are primarily impoverished, landless laborers and marginal farmers.

CARE
(www.care.org or +1-800-521-2273)
A leading humanitarian organization fighting global poverty, CARE places special emphasis on working alongside poor women because, equipped with the proper resources, women have the power to help whole families and entire communities escape poverty.

Esperanza
(www.esperanza.org or +1-425-451-4359)
Esperanza focuses on long-lasting solutions for families through microcredit, education and business training, vocational training, and health services. The organization works with community members, using culturally appropriate methods, such as baseball. Its activities are currently located in the Dominican Republic.

FINCA International
(www.villagebanking.org or +1-202-682-1510)
Launched in 1984, FINCA International provides microloans and related services through village banks in 21 countries throughout Latin America, Africa, and the newly independent states of Eastern Europe and Central Asia. FINCA serves people at all levels of poverty and has developed expertise in helping entrepreneurs in areas that are emerging from conflict.

Fonkoze
(www.fonkoze.org or +1-888-921-5726)
Fonkoze is a Haitian foundation that supports the organized poor, providing them with essential banking services and assist-

ing borrowers with literacy, business training, and health education. Fonkoze USA is the American nonprofit that assists Fonkoze in its work. Established in 1994, Fonkoze currently has over 90,000 depositors, more than 30,000 borrowers, and 26 branch offices in Haiti.

Freedom from Hunger
(www.freefromhunger.org or +1-800-708-2555)
Established in 1946 to fight hunger with innovative self-help programs, Freedom from Hunger has, since 1988, developed an integrated microloan, health, and nutrition program. Its Credit with Education program serves more than 350,000 families in some of the poorest countries.

Grameen Bank
(www.grameen-info.org)
Grameen Bank is one of the earliest microloan organizations and remains a microcredit leader. Founded by Professor Muhammad Yunus in 1976, it has 6.61 million borrowers, 97% of whom are women, with loans averaging less than $200 each. Grameen Bank's activities are concentrated in Bangladesh, but the organization is active in other countries as well. The Grameen Bank model favors a group lending methodology where members guarantee each other's loans.

Grameen Foundation
(www.grameenfoundation.org or +1-202-628-3560)
Grameen Foundation replicates grassroots lending programs using the Grameen Bank model. The organization helps serve 2.2 million borrowers and partners with 52 microfinance institutions in 22 countries. It seeks financial gifts, volunteer help, expertise, and contacts. Contributions can be directed to

microloan programs in any country where it works. Its Grameen Technology Center develops innovative technology to provide new opportunities for the poor. This organization was formerly named Grameen Foundation USA.

HOPE International
(www.hopeinternational.org or +1-717-464-3220)

HOPE International is a Christian nonprofit organization focused on building microfinance institutions in some of the most challenging environments in Africa, Asia, Eastern Europe, and the Caribbean. HOPE offers opportunities for short-term trips for donors to experience the effectiveness of microfinance firsthand. HOPE also focuses on the next generation of entrepreneurs through youth-focused business training, and actively partners with local churches. (*Note: several other unrelated organizations have similar names.*)

MEDA
(www.meda.org or +1-800-665-7026)

Mennonite Economic Development Associates, or MEDA, offers financial services to the poor as an expression of the Mennonites' long tradition of Christian social action. MEDA provides business-oriented economic development programs, including microcredit.

Opportunity International
(www.opportunity.org or +1-800-793-9455)

A global network of partner organizations, Opportunity International raises funds and implements microfinance programs for poor entrepreneurs in the developing countries of Latin America, Asia, Africa, and Eastern Europe. It popularized a group-lending methodology that it calls *trust banks*. Its

programs provide small business loans, training, counsel, and
other financial services. While it is one of the longest established microcredit organizations, dating from the 1970s, it is
also one of the most progressive. It was one of the first to set
up lending programs in Eastern Europe as well as sophisticated investment options for supporters who wish to loan as
well as donate money. In 2007 Opportunity expects to be serving 1 million clients in more than 30 countries.

SKS Microfinance
(www.sksindia.com)
SKS empowers the poor through microloans and other microfinance services. It concentrates its activities in certain states
in India and hopes to reach a milestone of 700,000 clients by
March 2007. SKS is growing very fast and is a leader in tech-
nological innovation and operational excellence.

Unitus
(www.unitus.com or +1-888-286-4887)
A nonprofit organization taking a hybrid approach to fighting
global poverty, Unitus uses strategies from the venture capital,
investment banking, and strategy consulting industries. It
partners with emerging microfinance institutions (MFIs),
structures investments for them, provides consulting services,
and exits when its partners achieve scale and capacity to grow.

Women's World Banking
(www.swwb.org or +1-212-768-8513)
Women's World Banking supports member organizations that
offer direct services to impoverished women. It helps affiliates
succeed as microfinance institutions and change agents by

providing tailored, integrated service in the areas of technical programs, financial products, policy change activities, and linkages and learning projects.

World Concern
(www.worldconcern.org or +1-800-755-5022)
A Christian humanitarian organization that provides emergency relief and community development in underdeveloped countries, World Concern helps more than 2 million people a year with disaster relief, job training, and microcredit.

World Relief
(www.wr.org or +1 800-535-5433)
World Relief began in the 1940s as the relief and development arm of the National Association of Evangelicals of the United States. The organization usually operates its programs in partnership with evangelical churches overseas. World Relief provides both disaster relief and development programs. Microcredit is one of its core development interventions.

World Vision
(www.worldvision.org or +1 888-511-6548)
A Christian humanitarian organization dedicated to working with children, families, and their communities, World Vision is well known for helping children by asking donors to directly sponsor them. In 2005, it made $169 million in microloans in 47 countries. Through its VisionFund, it uses sophisticated financial mechanisms to expand resources available for lending.

MICROCREDIT INFORMATION SOURCES

Selected Web Sites to Learn about Microcredit

The following Web sites are not directly affiliated with microcredit providers. Web sites of microcredit providers, such as those listed in Appendix B (especially Grameen Foundation), often contain excellent information. This is not meant to be an exhaustive list, but it contains those sites that Eric and Phil have found to be particularly informative.

www.ABillionBootstraps.com
This Web site includes information compiled after this book was published. Check for resources on poverty and microcredit. Also through this Web site you may contact the authors of *A Billion Bootstraps*, Phil Smith and Eric Thurman.

www.bouldermicrofinance.org

The Boulder Institute of Microfinance and a similar program at the University of New Hampshire listed below are the premier institutes where microfinance practitioners receive advanced in-service training. The resources section of its Web site contains a wide array of information on industry best practices.

www.cgap.org

CGAP has its origins in the World Bank and today is a consortium of 33 public and private development agencies working to expand access to microcredit. It serves development agencies, financial institutions, government policymakers, and other service providers. CGAP changed its name recently from Consultative Group to Assist the Poorest to Consultative Group to Assist the Poor. Time will tell whether over time this indicates mission drift from supporting programs for those who need microcredit most.

www.chalmers.org

The Chalmers Center for Economic and Community Development at Covenant College trains in methodologies that permit local groups to run microsavings and microlending programs with little or no assistance from large international groups. It is a popular resource for church-centered programs interested in economic development within low-income communities.

www.gdrc.org

The Global Development Research Center has a virtual library on microcredit.

www.ifmr.ac.in/cmf
The Centre for Microfinance based in India offers a wealth of practitioner training.

http://mdi-nh.org/
Microenterprise & Development Institute-New Hampshire and a similar study program in Boulder, Colorado, listed previously, are the premier study centers for advanced training in microfinance.

www.microcreditsummit.org
The Microcredit Summit Campaign has been on a nine-year promotion urging the microcredit movement to serve 100 million of the world's poorest families with credit for self-employment by the year 2005. At the end of 2005, it identified 3,133 microcredit institutions that were reaching more than 113 million clients. Not all those loans, however, were offered to the poorest families, so a second phase of the campaign is underway to reach even more people and go deeper into poverty. The Global Microcredit Summit 2006 was held in November 2006 in Halifax, Nova Scotia, Canada, attracting more than 2,000 delegates from more than 100 countries.

www.microfinancegateway.org
The Microfinance Gateway is a comprehensive online resource for the microcredit industry. It includes news, research and publications, resource centers, and organization and consultant profiles. It also has discussion groups and job listings. It is one of the busiest sites about microfinance on the Internet.

www.microlinks.org
microLINKS is a Web site created and run by the U.S. Agency for International Development (USAID). It provides information on microcredit, including lessons learned from USAID missions, partners, and practitioners.

www.mixmarket.org
The Microfinance Information eXchange (MIX) addresses one of the key challenges of the microfinance industry: the lack of reliable, comparable, and publicly available information on the financial strength and performance of microfinance institutions (MFIs), which underpins the development of a capital market for microfinance. It pursues its objectives through the *MicroBanking Bulletin* and the MIX (Microfinance Information eXchange) Market, which provides self-reported financial data on nearly 800 microfinance institutions, nearly 100 investors, and 140 partners.

www.peerservants.org
Peer Servants fosters Christian microfinance by training volunteers.

www.seepnetwork.org
SEEP Network is an organization of more than 67 private and voluntary organizations that support micro and small businesses in 139 countries and reach 23 million microentrepreneurs and their families.

www.themfmi.org
The Microfinance Management Institute advances the capacity of microfinance management worldwide.

www.uncdf.org/mfdl/index.php?_mode=students.home
The United Nations Capital Development Fund offers an online distance learning course about microfinance.

www.usaid.gov
USAID is the principal U.S. government agency to extend assistance to countries recovering from disaster, trying to escape poverty, and engaging in democratic reforms.

www.woccu.org
The World Council of Credit Unions, Inc. is an advocate and development agency for credit unions.

www.worldbank.org
The World Bank has numerous resources concerning poverty and microcredit.

www.yearofmicrocredit.org
This is the Web site for the U.N. International Year of Microcredit 2005. The objective of the program is to unite member states, U.N. agencies, and microfinance partners in building sustainable microfinance organizations. The Web site has an excellent resource library and database designed to raise public awareness and support for microcredit.

Books about Microcredit, Poverty, and Aid

Banker to the Poor: Micro-Lending and the Battle against World Poverty, Muhammad Yunus, PublicAffairs, Perseus Books Group, New York, N.Y., 1999.

The End of Poverty: Economic Possibilities for Our Time, Jeffrey D. Sachs, Penguin Books LTD, London, England, 2005.

Give Us Credit, Alex Counts, Times Books, a division of Random House, New York, N.Y., 1996.

Microfinance Handbook: An Institutional and Financial Perspective, Joanna Ledgerwood, The World Bank, Washington, D.C., 1999.

The Poor and Their Money, Stuart Rutherford, Oxford University Press, New Delhi, India, 2000.

The Road to Hell: The Ravaging Effects of Foreign Aid and International Charity, Michael Maren, The Free Press, New York, N.Y., 1997.

Walking with the Poor, Bryant L. Myers, Orbis Books, Maryknoll, N.Y., 2005.

The White Man's Burden: Why the West's Efforts to Aid the Rest Have Done So Much Ill and So Little Good, William Easterly, The Penguin Press, New York, N.Y., 2006.

CALCULATING AN END TO POVERTY

Phil Smith

I am an engineer by training and an executive and investor by profession. The left side of my brain works overtime. While I am emotionally involved with microcredit, my business instincts override my feelings. I want to run the numbers. My curiosity has driven me to create a formula that will show me what I am accomplishing when I give to a microcredit program. While I hear personal stories and enjoy them, I want to go beyond anecdotal accounts. I want to see the data. What does it really cost to change a single life using microcredit?

It is impossible, of course, to precisely calculate what it takes to help people lift themselves out of poverty, what we call, in this book, the cost-per-life ratio (CPL). The fact that we cannot have perfect precision in this calculation should not dissuade us from attempting to arrive at a reasonable approximation. I am convinced it is possible, while allowing for substantial variation, to compute what it costs to change a life using microcredit. If you are the kind of person who enjoys diving into the numbers, as I do, here are factors to use in such a calculation.

- *Total of loans.* In Chapter 5, I proposed a rule of thumb that the total amount of borrowed funds required to improve a microbusiness enough to move a borrower up the economic ladder is roughly equal to the average annual income per capita of the borrower's country (which is further defined to be GNI per capita 2005, Atlas method as shown in the World Development Indicators database, www.worldbank.org).
- *Recycling of loans.* Estimate how many times donations will circulate by being reloaned. As an example with six-month loans, after ten years the recycle rate is 20, which means the same money is used 20 times.
- *Multiple beneficiaries.* Recognize that a microbusiness supports an entire family. On average, assume families have five members.

The basic formula is simple. Multiply the recycle rate of 20 by 5, which is the number of family members. That means every donation directly changes the lives of 100 children and adults because of loan recycling. Then, the last step in the computation is to divide the country's average annual per capita income by 100 to calculate the cost per person. It turns out that the final CPL is exactly 1% of a country's average annual per capita income. If you do the math, you will quickly conclude, as I have, that the net cost is amazingly little to change the entire course of life for a poor person.

I invited my tough-minded business friends to debunk my formula if they could. Their incisive challenges came down to three issues.

1. "You say the average total amount of loans needed to move someone up the poverty ladder is 100% of the target country's average annual income per capita. What if a particular person or situation requires much more, such as three or four times that amount?"
2. "While almost 100% of borrowers pay back their loans, that does not necessarily mean each one moves up the poverty ladder."
3. "What if the lending organization isn't at breakeven yet? Doesn't that mean that it cannot recycle the whole amount of loans that are paid back? That has to deplete the amount of money available to lend."

These are excellent arguments. A fair calculation of the real cost to finance getting someone out of poverty must consider each of them.

At this point, my objective is not to debate the data, but to make certain the formula can accommodate all these important variables. Furthermore, there is nothing wrong with being conservative. For instance, you may want to assume that only half the people who repay loans actually rise out of poverty. It can be smart to be cautious, especially until you acquire enough direct experience to take a more aggressive stance. I will show how to modify the formula.

Percentage of Annual Income Adjustment

This part is easy. If you believe it will take more or less in total loans to help someone out of poverty, just increase or reduce the percentage up or down in the formula. If you think the amount needed is twice the annual average per capita income, use 2%; if you think the amount needed is triple, then 3%,; and so on. This factor may be influenced by location. For instance, urban areas might require higher loan amounts than rural areas.

Stuck in Poverty

To adjust for the possibility that not all borrowers are successful at escaping poverty, just factor that in as another adjustment. If you think the success ratio will only be one out of two borrowers, then multiply by 2/1 and the answer is 2%. If you think the success ratio is two out of three borrowers, then multiply by 3/2 and the answer is 1.5%. If you think the success ratio is four out of five borrowers, then multiply by 5/4 and the answer is 1.25%. This factor might be influenced by the level of poverty being attacked, the political situation, and other social factors.

Reuse of Loan Funds

Adjusting for the loan recycle rate is more complex but very important. It pays to examine this factor carefully. The more you study implications of the economic health of the lending organization, the more you will understand why sustainability is so vital.

If a program is truly sustainable or makes a profit, it theoretically costs nothing to bring people out of poverty. Here is an example. Imagine that five years ago a microcredit organization received a large donation which increased the amount it could loan. Since then, the organization moved above breakeven; all the costs to operate the program are less than what it takes in as interest from microloans. Six months ago, it lent $500 to a woman who has now just repaid the $500 in full and with interest. Her loan was the boost she needed to break free of poverty. By that we mean her family is healthy and eats regularly, her children are in school, and she has operating cash to continue her small business successfully. Technically, the cost to help that woman was zero. The organization already had the money and was recycling it. A viable lending program, like the one just described, can theoretically operate in perpetuity.

At the other extreme, an organization that is very young or has problems will operate below sustainability, which is the nonprofit way of saying it is losing money. That group must decapitalize its loan fund to keep going. Picture a very small program that has only $10,000 in its loan portfolio. Over six months, it has a shortfall of $1,000 when you compare interest earnings to expenses. The money now available to loan is only $9,000. That will yield even less interest earned with the next round of loans. The fund balance will slide by even more than another $1,000 during the next cycle. A trend line of declining sustainability is a serious matter. It quickly turns into crisis.

As I just explained, reloans are tied to sustainability. Understanding the pattern of reloans is essential. To see the pattern, you need a uniform time frame which you apply equally to any programs you evaluate. You can use any time period you wish as long as it is the same for any comparisons you are making. For my calculations, I fix the recycle period at ten years, and I assume six-month loans for a recycle figure of 20.

There is one further consideration: the size of the portfolio. The impact of a shortfall is diluted if the loan portfolio is large. For instance, if an organization lost $10,000 per year and its loan portfolio was $50,000, then the amount available to loan in the next cycle would be $40,000 and reloans would only be 80% of previous loans. If an organization lost $10,000 per year and its loan portfolio was $1 million, then the amount available to loan in the next cycle would be $990,000 or 99%.

I derived the table below, which gives you the factor to plug into the formula depending on the rate at which loans are recycled. For most situations, you will not want to invest in a microcredit program that has a follow-up loan rate below 80% unless the program is just getting started and is expected to improve quickly.

FOLLOW-UP LOAN RATE	FACTOR
100%	1.0
95%	1.5
90%	2.2
85%	3.1
80%	4.0

The Bottom Line

If you want to adjust for more than one of these variables, solving the formula below will compute the cost to change a life in a program you are thinking of supporting. As an example, assume that the program under examination needs to loan 200% of the country's average annual income per capita, only two out of three families that receive loans improve their lives significantly, and the program is able to reloan only 90% of the previous loans. These are the variables to use:

RT = the 1% rule of thumb

MA = the multiple of annual income needed as loans; in this example I use 2, for 200%

PE = poverty escape success or how many families get out of poverty; in this example we say two out of three or 3/2 which is 1.5 in the formula

RL = reloan rate, 90% in this example, which is a factor of 2.2 from the chart above

This is the formula:
RT × MA × PE × RL = CPL expressed as a percentage of the average annual income

This is the formula applied to the hypothetical program above:
1% × 2 × 1.5 × 2.2 = 6.6 % of the country's average annual income per capita

Now you have the cost-per-life as a percentage. Multiply that by the average annual income of the country. Two examples would be Ukraine with an average income of $1,520 or the Democratic Republic of Congo whose average is at $120. With a CPL percentage of 6.6%, as just calculated, that means the net cost of this program to free someone from poverty in Ukraine would be only $100.32, or only $7.92 in the Congo.

Even if my formula is off by a wide margin, which I do not believe it is, and it costs many times more than I have calculated to free people from poverty, it is still a bargain. Have you ever seen another system that actually dares to compute the real cost to change a life by helping people lift themselves from poverty? Put microcredit to the toughest possible scrutiny, and it passes the test.

Another Metric

For most of microcredit's history, an increase in personal income has been a key indicator of progress. Poor people leave poverty as their income rises, so the theory goes. While that is generally true, another metric is gaining attention. Building of assets is another important indicator of success. Lasting well-being comes as the poor gather assets such as savings accounts, equity in homes or land, successful businesses with higher income potential, and better job skills. These assets give borrowers realistic hope for a better future and the conviction that it will be attainable. Building assets is important for borrowers' long-term success, and this can be accomplished through the increase of both income and knowledge that microcredit provides.

Devastating poverty preys on half the people on Earth. They need programs to assist them when they suffer: additional nutrition, medical care, or some other humanitarian service. Even more, they need a way to break the grip of poverty. Once they have income and assets, they can provide for their own needs. Microcredit enables millions of people to lift themselves by their bootstraps.

NOTES

CHAPTER 1

1 *He has said, "Business can make* . . . David Kirkpatrick, "eBay's Founder Starts Giving;" *Fortune*, November 28, 2005.

1 *A Newsweek article explained the theory behind the gift* . . . Karen Breslau, "10 Big Thinkers for Big Business;" *Newsweek*, June 13, 2005.

5 *The headline of one small article caught my eye* . . . Rena Pederson, "What Will a $50 Loan Buy?" *Dallas Morning News*, November 9, 2003.

7 *Finally, Mariann handed me a Forbes magazine opened to an article* . . . Susan Kitchens, "Contrarian Charity;" *Forbes*, May 10, 2004.

10 *Innovators like the Omidyars* . . . Brad Pitt, interviewed on ABC's *Primetime Live*, August 2, 2005, noted the success of microfinance—small-loan programs that, as Pitt explained, "have a 95% or higher success rate" in creating self-sufficiency for the poor.

CHAPTER 2

16   *Buffett says* . . . Warren E. Buffett, Preface to the Fourth
Edition, *The Intelligent Investor* (New York: HarperCollins,
2005), p. ix.

16   *"Throughout this book the term will be used* . . ." Benjamin
Graham, *The Intelligent Investor* (New York: HarperCollins,
2005), p. 18.

16   *"Speculation is always fascinating* . . ." *ibid.,* p. 21.

17   *"Operations not meeting these requirements* . . ." Benjamin
Graham, *Security Analysis* (1934 ed.), pp. 55-56.

17   *"It is amazing to see how many capable businessmen* . . ."
Benjamin Graham, *The Intelligent Investor* (New York:
HarperCollins, 2005) p. 523.

18   *A Harris Interactive DonorPulse survey* . . . *The Harris Poll,*
no. 33, April 27, 2006.

18   *In their words, "81 percent of the Americans* . . . Paul C. Light,
Confidence in Charitable Organizations, Wagner Graduate
School of Public Service New York University,
August 2006.

20   *The study concluded, "Expressions of the benefit* . . . Philanthropy
in the News: An Analysis of Media Coverage,
FoundationWorks, 2006.

22   *Strong evidence suggests that the terms of the aid* . . .
"Causing Hunger: An Overview of the Food Crisis in Africa,"
Oxfam International, July 24, 2006.

24   *Listwin was determined to change that imbalance* . . .
www.canaryfoundation.org.

26 *The BBC and other reputable news organizations* . . . Angus
Stickler, "Brazil's Police 'Execute Thousands,'" *BBC News*,
November 23, 2005.

27 *This has led to the implausible situation* . . . *Nonprofit Overhead
Cost Project Brief*, Center on Philanthropy Indiana University,
February 2004.

28 *Only 35% said they felt charities* . . . Jane Lampman, "Rich to the
Rescue," *The Christian Science Monitor*, November 20, 2006.

29 *A New York Times editorial on Katrina contributions* . . .
"Re-examining the Red Cross," *New York Times*,
December 4, 2005.

CHAPTER 3

36 *While that is a laudable accomplishment* . . ." World Economic
Forum, Zurich, Switzerland, January 28, 2005, Sustainability
Forum, "Microcredit Grows Up."

36 *To highlight its importance in eliminating poverty* . . .
United Nations, www.uncdf.org/english/news_and_events/
newsfiles/20051207_state_of_microcredit.php.

37 *She now has many customers and is known* . . . www.hopeinte
national.org.

39 *In India, nine out of ten workers are in the informal sector* . . .
FINCA International, "The Global Picture," www.villag
banking.org/globalpic.htm.

40 *He points out that 2.5 billion people have never* . . . Connie
Bruck, "Millions for Millions," *New Yorker Magazine*,
October 30, 2006.

40   *With her new export/import business* . . . www.peerservants.org.

44   *"You can be middle class in your head . . ."* Thomas L. Friedman, *The World Is Flat* (New York: Farrar, Straus and Giroux, 2005).

CHAPTER 4

52   *With proof of progress in hand* . . . A composite story.

55   *Finally, to avoid having to invite him to stay* . . . Carol Stigger, *The Things I Left Behind*, unpublished manuscript.

57   *Today, Shanti is able to focus on growing* . . . Grameen Foundation USA, *Annual Report 2003*.

CHAPTER 5

68   *From a risked investment standpoint* . . . Information provided by Grameen International. Donor is anonymous by request.

71   *According to the World Bank, in 2005* . . . The World Bank, www.worldbank.org/data/databytopic/GNIPC.pdf : GNI per capita 2005, Atlas method.

CHAPTER 6

80   *Opportunity International clients also mentored and trained the young people* . . . www.habitat.org/ame/stories/pilot_projects_aids.aspx.

82   *By 2005, this Microcredit Plus program was serving* . . . www.freedomfromhunger.org/pdfs/Credit_w_Education_10-2005_12-2005.pdf.

84 *Fatoumata shares her wagon and new knowledge . . .*
www.freedomfromhunger.org/bytes/women.

CHAPTER 7

96 *In addition, they had reached deeper into poverty . . .* 2005
interview, name withheld by request.

100 *In 2006, John and Jacque Weberg announced . . .* www.
opportunity.org/site/pp.asp?c=7oIDLROyGqF&b=2073707.

100 *The other $5 million was pledged by Janet McKinley . . .* Elizabeth
Bernstein, "Loan Aid;" *Wall Street Journal,* June 5, 2005.

105 *The program achieved operational sustainability in 2005 . . .*
www.grameendelafrontera.org.

108 *It is remarkable that so many desperately want and can take
advantage . . .* Peter Brinkerhoff, HOPE Kisangani [Congo]
program office, July 14, 2005, as told to Dave Larson.

CHAPTER 8

111 *He might reply with . . .* Sun Tzu, *The Art of War,* translated
by Ralph D. Sawyer (Boulder, Col.: Westview Press, Inc.,
1994).

115 *Every hour, approximately 1,200 children within this group . . .*
2006 Annual Report, United Nations Development Program.

118 *The aim is to reach these goals by 2015 . . .* www.un.org/
millenniumgoals.

118 *According to the World Bank, "Progress in eradicating hunger . . .*
www.moe.gov.pk/MDGs/Millennium%20Development%20
Goals%20Malnutrition%20and%20Hunger.htm.

119 *The 1.2 billion people who eke out an existence* . . . American
Council for United Nations University, www.acunu.org/
millennium/Global_Challenges/chall-07.html.

121 *According to one UN estimate* . . . "No Place for Your
Daughters," *The Economist*, November 24, 2005.

122 *Of the 1.2 billion people who live on less than $1 a day* . . .
International Development Exchange,
www.idex.org/issue.php?issue_id=6.

123 *Her 15-year-old daughter, Fanta, is delighted* . . .
Nomsombougou Community Bank, a World Vision
microfinance partner in Mali.

124 *Those are results to celebrate because* . . . The Millennium
Development Goals 2005 Report,
http://unstats.un.org/unsd/mi/pdf/MDG%20Book.pdf.

CHAPTER 9

130 *On the first leg of the flight from Tulsa to Dallas-Fort Worth
airport* . . . Jim Stovall, *The Ultimate Gift* (Mechanicsburg,
Pa., Executive Books, April 2000).

CHAPTER 10

146 *According to the GivingUSA Foundation, Americans contributed
$260 billion in 2005* . . . www.aafrc.org/.

147 *Despite the recognition of microfinance as a proven poverty-
reduction tool* . . . *Tapping the Financial Markets for
Microfinance*, Grameen Foundation USA, 2005.

149 *To its credit, the Gates Foundation has built performance measurements* . . . "The New Powers of Giving," *The Economist*, July 1, 2006, p. 65.

151 *Like many people who are both successful and significant* . . . Jeff Rutts, HOPE International, 2005 interview, www.hopeinternational.org/_files/Builder2005.pdf.

155 *Even my mother moved me along in my quest* . . . Renata J. Rafferty, *Don't Just Give It Away* (Worcester, Mass.: Chandler House Press, 1999).

GLOSSARY

Terminology is a continuing debate in the microcredit movement. Some practitioners use terms differently from the way we have in this book. Some will mix terms interchangeably or apply them with various nuances. Throughout the text of this book, the authors use the general term microcredit *when other, more technical language, would also fit.*

Community Banks, Trust Banks or Village Banks   The method used most often to dispense microcredit and related services. These function as small, community credit unions. In most cases borrowers and borrower groups coguarantee loans. In many of these groups, the borrowers also perform most of the loan administration.

Microcredit   Microloans and any other form of small credit.

Microcredit Plus   The term used by the authors to describe situations where any other financial, business development, or social service is provided along with microloans.

Microenterprise Development (MED)   Microfinance activities with the addition of business development services such as training, marketing, and market intelligence, which are primarily used to develop a borrower's microbusiness. Services could also include social intermediation skills such as group interaction skills, leadership training, and group learning.

Microfinance   This is a broader category than microcredit. It includes microloans and other financial services such as savings and insurance.

Microfinance Institutions (MFIs)   Formal, government-registered financial organizations that provide microloans and may provide other MED functions to borrowers. In short, attaining MFI status often means becoming a bank. MFIs must provide adequate administration services and also raise money to fund all of their activities. MFIs can be nongovernmental organizations, savings and loan cooperatives, government banks, or commercial banks.

Social Services   Services that may be included in addition to the microcredit process. These may include literacy training, health and nutrition skills, and faith-sharing activities. Provision of these social services may be a major goal of lenders and/or borrowers.

INDEX

ABOUT THE AUTHORS

Phil Smith is a private investor, estate administrator, and advocate for microcredit and retirement issues. He writes and speaks under the banner Practicing Significance. He is on the boards of directors of Eagle Rock Energy and several privately owned companies. He was formerly CEO and chairman of Prize Energy Corp. and Tide West Oil Company and a director of Pioneer Natural Resources Company and HS Resources, Inc. He can be contacted at PhilipBSmith@sbcglobal.net.

Eric Thurman is one of the world's leading experts in international philanthropy. He is president of Protos Fund and former CEO of Geneva Global Inc., where he supervised grant-making in more than half of the countries worldwide. He is a popular public speaker and appears frequently in news interviews, which recently included the *Financial Times*, *Forbes*, the *Wall Street Journal*, *Newsweek*, *Time*, and CNN. He has extensive experience directing microcredit programs. Earlier in his career as CEO of Opportunity International and HOPE International he managed poverty lending programs in more than 30 countries. He can be contacted at EThurman@ProtosFund.org.